CLONE C

CLONE CITY

Crisis and Renewal in Contemporary Scottish Architecture

MILES GLENDINNING

AND

DAVID PAGE

Polygon
Edinburgh

RCAHMS

© Miles Glendinning and David Page, 1999

Polygon
22 George Square, Edinburgh

Typeset in Bodoni and Helvetica
by Pioneer Associates, Perthshire, and
printed and bound in Great Britain by
The Cromwell Press, Trowbridge

A CIP record for this book is available from
the British Library

ISBN 0 7486 6255 3 (paperback)

The Publisher acknowledges subsidy from

THE SCOTTISH ARTS COUNCIL

towards the publication of this volume.

To link the Autumn of our own age with an approaching Spring, and pass, through Decadence, towards Renascence.[1]

Contents

The Authors   ix

Acknowledgements   x

1   AN EMPTY VESSEL?:
The Scottish City in Postmodern Space   1

2   *ARBOR SAECULORUM*:
An Archaeology of Utopian Confrontation   11

    The Historicist Age   15
    The Modernist Age   28
    The Postmodern Age   45
    A Monumental History: The Modernity
       of Heritage   54

3   BUILDING A DEMOCRACY:
A Reconciliation of People   63

    Return of the Prophets   66
    Towards a Neotechnic Society   77
    Education and Environment   84
    Aristo-democratic Citizens: The Ennoblement
       of Consumption and Production   90
    State of Order   98
    The Rebirth of Planning   103

4   CLYDEFORTH: Conurbation in Landscape   113
    Taming the Conurbation   119

Contents

5   CENTRES OF LIFE:
    Eutopian Cities of Tomorrow   137
    Brown Belts and Green Centres   146
    Inner Centres: Tyranny of the Tenement   150
    In-between Centres: Chaos of the Cul-de-sac   165

6   CITY PLACES – East and West   177
    New Towns: From Ideal to Place   177
    Old Towns in New Spaces: Re-imagining
        the Forth Valley   186
    Black Holes and Borders: The Resurrection
        of the Clyde Valley   194
    Border-cities   208

7   CONCLUSION: Monuments to the Future   217

    Notes   225

    List of Illustrations   228

    Index   232

The Authors

Miles Glendinning Horsey is a writer and historian. He works at RCAHMS, where he heads the Topographical and Threatened Buildings survey and publication programmes; and he teaches at the Department of Social Policy, University of Edinburgh. Recent publications which he has co-authored or edited include *Tower Block* (winner of the Alice Davis Hitchcock Medallion), *A History of Scottish Architecture* and *Building a Nation*; books on *Scotland's Parliaments* and the history of the housebuilding industry are forthcoming.

David Page is an architect and urbanist commentator. As a partner in Page & Park, he has co-designed a number of critically acknowledged works, including the Italian Centre and masterplans for Homes for the Future, Strathclyde University and Gorbals East, Glasgow. Current projects include the Lighthouse (Glasgow 1999), the Museum of Scottish Country Life, and the Centre for Contemporary Arts, Glasgow. He is a member of the Royal Fine Art Commission for Scotland and an Honorary Professor of Architecture at Edinburgh College of Art.

Acknowledgements

This book was originally envisaged as a publication about the new works and thoughts of contemporary Scottish architects' practices. In the course of our discussions with these firms, we became convinced that before a book of that kind could properly be written, a more urgent initial task was to challenge the global commodification which constrains all Scottish designers. The result was the present volume, a polemical and generalised rather than descriptive and specific book. Despite this change of approach, our discussions with these practices nevertheless formed the essential foundation for *Clone City*, although they are not in any way responsible (or to blame!) for the arguments which follow in these pages. The firms which helped us were the following: Arcade Architects; Benson & Forsyth; Davis Duncan; Elder & Cannon; Douglas Forrest; Malcolm Fraser; Richard Gibson; Graven Images; John Hope; McGurn, Logan, Duncan & Opfer; E. & F. McLachlan; McNeish Design; Richard Murphy; Allan Murray; David Murray Associates; NBA; Nicoll Russell Studios; Reiach & Hall; RMJM; Simister Monaghan; Simpson & Brown; Ben Tindall; and Ungless & Latimer.

More generally, we would like to thank our partners, families and colleagues for their forbearance during the past two years. We would also like to thank the following individuals for their specific assistance (including the supply of information or illustrations and the reading of text) or more general help or inspiration: Mark Baines; Alison Blamire; Bill Brogden; Tim Byram-Wigfield; Colin Campbell; Ian Campbell; Nicola Carr; Tom Connolly; Cairns Craig; Roger Emmerson; Suzanne Ewing; Graham Forbes; John Gibbons; Neil Gillespie; Hubert-Jan Henket; Richard Holloway; Graeme Hutton; Alan Johnston; Rob Joiner; Gus Lamb;

Acknowledgements

Neil Lamb; Elspeth Latimer; Joeran Lindvall; Eleanor MacAllister; Murdo MacDonald; Stuart MacDonald; Ranald MacInnes; Charles McKean; Aonghus MacKechnie; David MacRitchie; Jim Mackie; Lady Matthew and Aidan Matthew; Malcolm Mitchell; Chris Mummery; Diana Murray; Stefan Muthesius; Stuart Nichol; Miles Oglethorpe; Brian Park; David Paton; Chris Platt; Charles Prosser; Eva Rudberg; Roan Rutherford; Margaret Simpson; Fiona Sinclair; Paul Stallan; Gavin Stamp; Geoffrey Stell; Fraser Stewart; Sandy Stoddart; Paul Sutton; Sebastian Tombs; Steve Wallace; William Fraser Watt; Diane Watters; Volker Welter; David Whitham; and Ole Wiig.

The generous assistance of RCAHMS towards the cost of illustrations is gratefully acknowledged.

HERITAGE PARK

SALES OFFICE OPEN

2pm - 5pm

CALL S

Welcome to

HOUSING SITE OF 2.25 ACRES
CONSENT FOR 8 UNITS

9 SCREEN MULTIPL
BINGO CLUB, DISCO
AMERICAN BAR DINER &
DRIVE-THRU BURGER RESTA
UNITS

ous developmen
executive homes

SALES OFF

1

AN EMPTY VESSEL?
The Scottish City in
Postmodern Space

The jail might have been the infirmary, the infirmary might have been
the jail, the town-hall might have been either, or both, or anything
else, for anything that appeared to the contrary in the graces of their
construction. Fact, fact, fact everywhere in the material aspect of the
town; fact, fact, fact everywhere in the immaterial . . . A town so sacred
to fact, and so triumphant in its assertion, of course got on quite well?
Why, no, not quite well.[2]

In the closing years of this century, the Scottish urban environment
seems to have descended into a state of utter confusion. Today we
are experiencing a proliferation of patterns and forms unrelated
to each other, or even actively in conflict, to the point where it
becomes difficult to construct or even conceive of coherent relationships of buildings, people and places.

On all sides, there are the most glaring polarisations and
contradictions. In the general physical development of the city,
we witness a process of anarchic fragmentation and individualism,
especially in its chaotic peripheral spread. Yet alongside this, there
is a strange and pervasive regimentation, both in the way in which
each new development creates its own introverted and segregated
space, and in the way in which that introversion is legitimised by
the intensely controlled, isolated islands of conservation zones.
The historic centres and the 'traditional, dense' nineteenth-century
areas seem to be at war with the sprawling edge cities around
them, yet the enclave formula is common to both. More generally,
there appears to be an overriding homogenisation, breaking down
local or regional differences with standardised formulae, whether
business park or residential cul-de-sac. The result is a jumble of

1

segregated and standardised 'products' and areas, in competition with one another but linked together by a privatised transport network, whose tentacles extend far into the country; a combination of materialistic order with spatial anarchy. The bustlingly variegated uniformity of the individual 'facts' coexists with a chaotic splintering of the entire built environment.

As a whole, the 'meaning' of the city and its buildings, the correspondence between built patterns and their representation in ideas, seems polarised to the point of dissolution. On the one hand, there is an architecture of unbridled image, a vision made possible by the unrestrained, computer-aided production of electronic form and space; a vision of isolated prestige buildings, gestures of pure form conceived as the built 'signatures' of master designers; a vision of heroic, self-referential brilliance turning its back on the everyday world around it. And on the other hand, there is an architecture of unbridled fact and production, determined solely by the calculations of engineering design, construction output and marketing profit: where business is needed, metal sheds spring up, planned on a single storey to encourage economy or selling motivation; where homes are needed, lines of small brick boxes march into view, always different yet always the same, whether in city, suburb or country: standard units of living-consumption and pre-structured 'life-style choice'; and sprouting everywhere at the interstices are innumerable smaller 'facts', such as the ceaselessly proliferating transmitter masts of rival mobile-phone companies.

In this environment of fragments and mirrors, nothing is what it seems. 'Choice' can mean standardised order, 'public realm' privatised space, 'traditional community' scattered newness, 'holistic sustainability' laissez-faire opportunism, and 'park' a wasteland of cars and supermarkets: retail park, leisure park, business park, theme park. Everywhere we look we see images of care and variety in a sea of unordered homogeneity. For example, the Image of Heritage, a layer of carefully controlled 'oldness' pasted across a reality of commercialised newness. Or the Image of Scottishness, a veneer of solidarity cast across torn-up roots.

And the Mask of Village Community, a facade of 'mixed use' and 'place' hiding uniformity and segregation: every building or project a similar microcosm of 'variegated city'; an urban structure broken down into bite-size chunks, introverted clusters of defensible space; a unique formula that can be applied everywhere and anywhere, allowing peripheral urban extensions, council housing scheme regenerations, housing areas in New Towns, even multiplex leisure complexes to be hailed as 'urban villages'.

We realise from these conflicts of meaning that this is not just a problem of visual disorder but also a social and ethical issue. What is in question is not only the environments themselves but the system that produces them. To put it in a single sentence: what we are seeing is a denial of any critical vision for the spatial ordering of change.

Nobody seems to have either the power or the motivation to try to bring together these fragments, to reconcile conflicting demands through collective ideals. Thus the city and its makers can do no more than react passively to outside 'reality', either reflecting it or escaping from it in fantasies, but in all cases fearfully submitting to the flow of the market. Everything is absorbed into the commercial process. With citizens as atomised consumers, and with 'experts' and intellectuals dethroned from any special pretensions of prestige, the traditional authoritative and critical voices are stilled. Many intellectuals have stepped back completely from active critical commentary. Irvine Welsh's addicts, in their nihilistic withdrawal, are part of the same atomised society as the isolated clusters of brick box homes. Nor does state authority play a norm-setting role any longer. Many municipal and central bodies have now become more and more like development companies, furiously competing for investment.

For building designers, too, today's conditions imply a loss of vocation. Whether dedicated to image or production, the common underlying direction of design seems to be that of a technical support for selling and consumption, with the greatest contribution coming from a new, factual ruling class of the Scottish built environment, the engineers and marketing consultants with their

3

concern for the rote application of standards, and the calculation of profits. Under their impetus, things are driven ever 'forward' with incredible dynamism and 'progress' continues unabated, but with no other governing idea than material accumulation. These groups themselves are simply doing their jobs, conscientiously and dutifully, within an empty space created by us all.

As a critical community, we have mentally evacuated this everyday environment, while continuing to occupy it physically and continuing to consume it at a level of basic material adequacy. On the surface, there is bustle and solidity; beneath, a kind of emptiness and silence. Commissioned to design a Scottish pavilion in 1991 for an international architectural exhibition in Leeuwarden, architect Allan Murray and artist Alan Johnston dramatised this schism in the monumental yet hollow design of their tower, with a 'translucent inner void at the heart of the perceptually solid construction'. This metaphorical image, its form inspired by Robert Adam's eighteenth-century monument to David Hume on Edinburgh's Calton Hill, was conceived as a Scottish contribution to a wider international debate. For our predicament in Scotland forms part of an international phenomenon, a globalist market society, with its unfettered flows of information and money, currents whose potential unpredictability and blind destructiveness have recently been felt right across the world.

This market ethos has its own special form of expression in the field of culture. The name for the culture of the global marketplace is 'postmodernity'. Its characteristics were summed up as long ago as 1984 by the cultural critic Fredric Jameson – using architecture as an illustration or metaphor – as a regime of unending layers of fetishistically seductive surfaces or images, an alienating and disorientating labyrinth which draws us in further and further, and destroys all certainties. Within architecture, 'Postmodernism' is nowadays complacently seen as a restricted stylistic movement of the 1980s, a movement now successfully rejected and relegated to the status of a past bogeyman. But in reality, the wider cultural movement of postmodernity continues to expand today, alongside global capitalism, and embraces architecture alongside all other strands of culture. <u>Architecture is in reality ever more involved with the world of commodified image-making,</u> through computer-generated space and the promotion of a global traffic in the reputation and work of architect superstars.

In present-day Scotland, the threatening implications of postmodernity's continuing processes of disorientation and evacuation have been summed up most sensationally in the startling developments claimed in the technology of cloning – an advance in scientific 'progress' which potentially brings in its wake huge material benefits but at the same time opens up previously unimaginable moral and social conflicts. Through this trumpeted feat of Scottish ingenuity, what was once unique threatens to become the subject of mass reproduction; and relationships which were previously seen as fixed are potentially scrambled into bizarre permutations of past and future. Everything, including what was once personal and private, as well as the public rule of the state, now may come under the rule of commodified 'lifestyle choice'.

Cloning is the ultimate symbol of regimentation and anarchy at the same time; the fact that some of its advances may arguably be copywriters' hyperbole rather than reality only accentuates that symbolic status within postmodern culture. The issue highlighted by the sensationalised debate over cloning is the issue which is at the heart of this book: the issue of identity. If the uncontrolled cloning of individual animals or human beings would encroach on personal identity, then Clone City – the city formed by the mindless, market-driven proliferation of built environments – represents a corresponding threat to our collective identity. After all, 'made' objects and people are mutually constructed: we make *them*, but they help *us* to order our existence. This constant interaction is especially powerful in architecture, because of buildings' sheer size, complexity and enduring character. Here it operates at several levels, which range from the individual personality to the collective and impersonal power of institutions and states.

Today, in the wake of the momentous progress of the home-rule cause during 1997, the issue of expression of identity in Scotland is once more of burning prominence and is closely bound up with the political debates about Scottish democracy. In other words, what can a 'renewal of democracy' in one particular country possibly mean for the citizen or the community, in an era of globally controlled capitalism combined with rampant individualism? Up to now, the architectural contribution to that debate has focused almost solely on the siting and design of Scotland's new parliament building. But is it not a contradiction in terms to limit discussion of 'democratic architecture' to a single building, however important, if the entire built environment is in a state of disorientation around it? In other areas of the country's culture, concerted critiques of the effects of globalisation and postmodernity have begun, questioning the dumbing down of issues of Scottish identity by 'Scotland the Brand'. Today's debates about the parliament building, with their focus on signature designers, and their polarisations of simplified values, such as tradition versus modernism or 'Scottishness' versus internationalism, show that architecture has not yet joined in those wider debates. It is still confined within a postmodern world of images and 'lifestyle choice'.

Democracy is nothing if it is not concerned with the whole nation. This book is about a national crisis of the built environment, and how, by attempting to solve it, we can in turn contribute to the democratic process. It is not a contradiction in terms that the book is concerned with only one area of the country, the Central Belt, embracing the Clyde and Forth Valleys and, with them, the bulk of urban Scotland. There are other environments of equal importance to Scottish identity, above all the rural axis stretching from the Borders to the Highlands and Islands, but the built environment is among the least of the problems of those areas. And there are other urban centres, such as Dundee or Aberdeen, which share some of Clone City's features of crisis, but in an isolated form. But only in the Central Belt has the crisis of Clone City developed into an interrelated crisis of the entire urban system. For urban Scotland, the national crisis is the same thing as the crisis of the Central Belt. It is the threat of the apparently uncontrolled spread of Clone City in the Central Belt, not the design of the parliament house, which should be seen as the most important urban architectural issue of Scottish democratic renewal. If we as a society can succeed in controlling and transforming the 'clone' represented by uncontrolled urbanisation in the Central Belt, then we will have established a powerful conduit of active involvement in the democratic process. If we fail, then our continuing addiction to the narcotic forces of the global marketplace will have been once more demonstrated.

This analysis, so far, takes us no further than a state of critical perplexity. It makes it clear that we have arrived at a situation of intolerable crisis and confusion. But it does not explain why or how this has happened, or begin to suggest how we can escape from it. The main purpose of this book is not to make destructive criticisms, even of the particular built forms which happen to make up today's Clone City, but to use polemic as a stimulus to positive ideas for the future. In this first chapter, we have presented Clone City's environments in a sensational and exaggerated form. But in many ways, the remainder of the book is an attempt to qualify that polemical formulation, to argue for a considered, long-term solution rather than a short-term reflex reaction. The central argument of this book is that today's Clone City is a symptom, rather than the disease itself. It will not be enough just to cure the symptom, for instance by forbidding the building of brick clone homes – intolerable though they are – or by changing architectural style, whether to 'modern' or 'traditional' or anything else, or by using signature architects. The underlying problem is the general way in which we in Scotland conceive of our built environment, and its development; the way that, at the moment, we passively accept what is handed to us.

Accordingly, this book is not a 'manual of good design', a 'survey of contemporary progressive Scottish architecture' or a 'conspectus of sociological trends'. It is not written specifically for architects or designers, so much as for the patrons and occupiers of buildings and for the citizens of the Scottish city in general. It is an appeal to all those involved in sustaining and inhabiting the city to take a careful look at the way in which we discuss those activities. It accompanies the reader on a step-by-step exploration, proceeding gradually deeper from the most general historical and social aspects to more practical issues of city planning. Even then, it does not offer detailed, specific prescriptions, but sets out a more general manifesto of hope, a pointer to a long-term strategy of resistance and recovery from mindless materialism. Only in that way, rather than by ephemeral image changes, will architecture be able to make a real, enduring contribution to the building of the new Scottish democracy: in the words of that past prophet of the Scottish city, Patrick Geddes, 'to link the Autumn of our own age with an approaching Spring, and pass, through Decadence, towards Renascence.'[1]

2

ARBOR SAECULORUM
An Archaeology of
Utopian Confrontation

I believe this is the historical Age, and this the historical Nation.[3]

If we content ourselves with simply denouncing and rejecting the
spatial forms of today's Clone City and replacing them with other,
radically different ones, we will get nowhere. Indeed, we will be
in a worse situation than ever. The underlying problem is not the
architectural forms assumed by today's chaos, but the underlying
systems of ideas which have produced them. Clone City is not, in
its essence, a set of forms, but the result of a process, a way of
conceptualising the development of the city in historical time
which relies on violent confrontations, polarisations over time
and over place. It is a way of coping with social and economic
change by repeatedly and forcefully seizing control and changing
direction, bulldozing through history, leaving a debased residue on
either side; a process whose aggression and compartmentalisation
was well suited to the society of past centuries, but which has
become paralysed and fragmented by its own latent self-contradic-
tions in recent decades. In trying to unravel the crisis of identity
in today's city for the sake of the future, we have to begin by looking backwards. We have to begin by defining and describing a
historical process – one which has combined within itself both
cultural and architectural change.

   In the Western or developed world, architecture enjoys a
complex and paradoxical relation to society in general. On the
one hand, because of its sheer size and the investment it requires,
it must always, by definition, broadly express the aspirations of
the ruling power. An anti-establishment architecture is almost a

contradiction in terms. Yet, on the other hand, because of its abstract nature and enduring materials, architecture must also necessarily look beyond the ephemeral concerns of the moment. There is a constant impulse to refer to higher motives or ideal forms, to assume that it must serve a higher goal than itself. A directly and exclusively 'realist' or 'political' architecture is both impracticable or implausible.

Thus architecture is always committed and detached at the same time. An architecture without a value system is impossible to imagine. In fact, a very complex value system is always necessary to encompass all its conflicting demands. This ambiguous relation of architecture and life was embodied in the first and most enduring system of architectural values, enunciated in antiquity by Vitruvius. Vitruvius argued that there was no one privileged architectural value, but instead a balance between three, the 'Vitruvian triad': *uenustas* (visual beauty), *firmitas* (constructional solidity) and *utilitas* (usefulness). It is in that balance that architecture's critical, active relation to the outside world has resided and still resides today. The triad also provides a way of dealing with historical change: the balance is readjusted or expressed in different forms to reflect the changing external contraints on architecture. In its first millennium and a half, that framework evolved at a relatively sedate pace. But in the last two to three centuries, historical change took on a different character, one that challenged the Vitruvian triad far more directly.

These have been the centuries of modernisation, a time of incessant social, economic and architectural transformation, in which history itself has taken on a dynamic and driving form. Over these centuries, the main driving force has been the impulse of freedom, especially personal and individual freedom. Freedom from the necessity to do things as they have always been done; freedom from the tyranny of compulsory community; freedom from grinding subsistence work and from disease. This process of individual liberation has spread to ever wider and wider sections of society; but as it has done so, it has incessantly brought disruption in its train, disruption that has had to be collectively regulated,

12

sometimes by the most severe methods, in order to bring about some reintegration. The story of modern society is in many ways the story of a running battle between these twin elements of modernity – the impulse of freedom and individuality on the one hand, and the restraint of order and collectivity on the other.

This is a universal Western story. But it is also a story in which Scotland has played a special role, because modernity in this country has such long roots. Ever since the seventeenth century, and especially from the late eighteenth century onwards, Scotland has been a 'historical nation' characterised by continual, radical transformations. Only England, France and, perhaps, Germany and the United States could be said to have a similarly long and complex history of modernity; and those were much larger societies in which its impact could be dispersed. Scotland has been a concentrated laboratory for radical experiments of change, experiments given an additional force up to the mid-twentieth century because of the country's special commitment to the building of British imperialism, with all its energy and sense of messianic mission. Here, we could expect to find the most iconoclastic and ruthless solutions.

In this process, the role of the built environment has been a complicated one, owing to its ambiguous relationship to the ruling power at any stage. Because of its own material solidity, its representational role has naturally been concentrated on the side of order and stability. But because of buildings' own independent material reality, this has at the same time been a detached, critical order, all the time trying to balance the immediate pressures of the system, the shifting values of modernity, against architecture's own, Vitruvian value system of beauty, solidity and usefulness. The role of architecture, in post-eighteenth-century Scotland as in all other countries undergoing violent modernisation, has been to find ways of organising space which can express change in an ordered way. This has been done by a constant process of renegotiation of the Vitruvian triad, trying to hold the critical balance through combinations of forms and meanings, trying to hold a line of consistency for long enough for the process of building and city planning, with their long lead times, to express a coherent outcome. The result has been 'identity' – created by the struggles to ennoble change, to fuse emotion and reason, to express the poetic out of the practical, and to reconcile freedom and order in constantly evolving circumstances. Architecture has not just mirrored society, but has actively provided the material backbone of our society's evolving identity.

Within Western civilisation as a whole, and especially in Scotland, that process of renegotiation and critical interrogation did not proceed in a smooth line, but convulsively, through violent reaction and counter-reaction. Because of the scale of the built environment, and its innate tendencies of inertia, each phase of architecture assumed a roller-coaster trajectory. It would begin with the construction of a complete Utopian ideal vision, integrating all the Vitruvian qualities. And it would then proceed inexorably to the stage of massed building of that formula under mounting social and economic pressure, leading to an exhaustion of debate and intellectual input, the splintering and polarisation of its elements, and their reproduction on a vast scale, divorced from any controlling sensibility. The inevitable critical reaction would, in turn, take a pent-up and explosive form, an anguished cry of alienation, sameness, emptiness, a call for total upheaval and for the harnessing of change through a radically new Utopian total vision, involving the abandonment or surgical remodelling of the newly rejected existing environments, whether types or specific areas. Often the next Utopia would be bolstered by praise of the alleged wholeness of a period in the far past, sometimes an era newly rehabilitated in its turn from previous disgrace. This endless clashing of Utopias was a creative and exciting, but also a destructive and repetitive process.

Thus Clone City, far from being the unique spawn of an unprecedented urban breakdown of the late twentieth century, is revealed as a key metaphor for architectural change in the immediately past centuries, a metaphor which refers to the stage of frenzied, fragmented reproduction of a Utopia about to be overthrown. It could almost stand as a generic name for the repeated architectural crises of modernity up to now, both in Western society in general, but also in Scotland in particular. What is different about our position today, as we will see, is that the cycle of violent advocacy and rejection, once so vital and creative, has now reached a stage of self-cancelling contradictions. This position demands a paradoxical remedy, whose radicalism would lie in its very break from the old radical remedies of rejection.

Doubtless, one of the reasons for this self-contradiction and exhaustion in the processes of architectural change has been the general turning away of society, in the most recent decades, from warlike and exclusionary patterns. Within architecture, this trend was reflected in the sudden rise to ascendancy of more inclusive, less confrontational ideas, building cumulatively on the past rather than violently rejecting it. These were expressed in a series of new movements of the 1970s, including user participation and conservation. Yet because of the continuing confrontational framework of architectural debate, these movements have been popularised up to now in a highly polemical, combative form: a contradictory and rather paralysing situation. Out of this gridlock, however, can ultimately come an understanding of the underlying processes at work, and the possibility and necessity of a change in them. That possibility is implicit even in the concept of Clone City itself. After all, the idea of the clone contains two elements: the initial structural copy, and the individual that results from the effects of environment and rearing. No two clones will end up as identical individuals. In the knowledge that previous generations of Utopian confrontations have seen the revaluation and creative use of building types and environments once branded as clones, such as the nineteenth-century tenement, can we approach our own problematic environments of today, our marketplace exurbias and our heritage Disney zones, in a similar spirit of creative renewal?

THE HISTORICIST AGE

The first step to resolving our present-day crisis of Clone City, then, is an 'archaeological dig' on the site, to reveal the previous layers of crises and attempted solutions. Here we need to be careful not to over-simplify the complications of reality. Although we talk about a cycle of Utopias, Clone City debasements and rejections, in fact the history of architecture shows a bewildering variety of movements, debates and policies. Certainly, there is nothing which exactly presages today's Clone City.

The architecture of modern Scottish society has gone through three main phases: that of late eighteenth and nineteenth-century capitalism, that of twentieth-century social democracy and finally that of the revived market liberalism of today. Architecturally, we can label these the Historicist, Modernist and Postmodern Ages. Each era was punctuated and separated by cloning controversies and attempted remedies. In each case, the process of Utopian rejection was driven by a rejection or problematisation of the city as it had been conceived by the previous phase: there were successive rejections of the old burgh, the industrial city and the replanned social-democratic city. Now, if the process of accusation were to continue, the polycentric city region would be in our target sights, were we to respond to the crisis of Postmodernity in a similar polemical fashion.

The Historicist Age itself began with the first of the major ruptures of historical modernity: the breaking apart of the society and architecture of aristocratic, feudal rule. Its focal building types – the country house and the royal burgh, with its tolbooth and church – were given unity and authority by the international architectural prestige of classical antiquity and the stone monumentality of the Scottish stone building tradition. But the number of buildings involved, the scale of architecture, was tiny by comparison with what was to come: to speak of 'cloning' in this context would be absurd. By the end of the eighteenth century and the beginning of the nineteenth, the oligarchic rule of lairds, ministers and burghers was no longer sustainable in the face of the onrush of urbanisation and industrialisation. Scotland launched with vigour into the quest for a constructed future of 'progress', involving both capitalistic 'Improvement' at home and commitment to the construction of the British empire overseas. The ruling framework was history, by which was meant as much the future, or destiny, as the past. A new urban middle class, calling for an individualistic liberal society, pushed the old rulers aside in a series of blows which culminated in the Disruption of the established Church of Scotland in 1843.

Urban life was shaped by a growing diversity of groups and activities, demanding more and more specialised buildings. And the method of building the city was shaped by the industrial capitalist processes that were gaining strength, and by the increasingly forceful pattern-making attitudes of colonialism and plantation which were bound up with British imperialism. There was the potential for repetitive mass building at scales ranging from building components up to entire city districts. In contrast to the contemporary Continent and to the later Scottish experience of the twentieth century, there was no attempt by the State to direct these processes. The main initiative was private, with public intervention limited almost exclusively to the municipalities, heirs to the pre-1707 royal burghs, with their semi-autonomy from the state.

Architecturally, the old, closed patrician patterns were co-opted and opened out: the old, simple hierarchies were replaced by new, more complicated ones. Of course, by twentieth-century standards, Scotland still remained a highly hierarchical and unequal society. Not only were the harmony and integration it achieved concentrated on a relative minority, but they were also achieved at a cost to many of those below. On the one hand, the structures of order balanced the protection of existing privilege against the gradually increasing spending power of the lower classes. Dean of Guild (building control) rules maintained the homogeneous monumentality of middle-class suburban develop-ment while at the same time bringing rapidly rising housing standards to the skilled working class. But, on the other hand, at the same time, many lived in 'made-down' shack-like dwellings completely outside the scope of formal architecture. The country house, as transformed by William Burn, was almost a microcosm

17

Hopetoun House

New Lanark

of this nineteenth-century city, with its combination of elite informality in the public and family quarters, and repressive supporting social order in the service zones. And the whole of society was supported by the external economic power of British imperialism, whose traditions of planned and segregated colonial settlement were shaped by, and in turn influenced, city planning 'at home'. By comparison with today's Clone City, with its disconnected image buildings, this more harshly unequal society was able to maintain an ordered relationship between the broad mass of new building and the elite masterpieces of architects such as Playfair and Adam. The social scope of architecture was much wider than before but many others were still left outside altogether.

Despite the materialistic and coercive aspects of this age of 'Improvement', this was no blind scramble for wealth. It was structured, alongside its materialism, by powerful collective ideals of the city as a common possession: a metaphoric, biblical vision of urban life, as a struggle to build a City on a Hill. We should bear in mind that the general reinforcement of religious fervour in the nineteenth century had developed the latent tendency of Scottish Calvinism to insinuate its philosophy of individual self-redemption into wider social, secular movements of advancement. That is not to say, of course, that society was united in some unified pilgrimage – far from it. In fact, what was so special was the attempt to reconcile such a diverse and forcefully liberal-individualist world outlook with an overarching emphasis on metaphysical ideals. In contrast to some other countries, such as Belgium or the United States, unstructured individualism and privatism has never been the dominant philosophy of Scottish society or architecture. Even in times of the most enthusiastic laissez-faire capitalism, the built environment was always regulated by ordering ideals.

This parallel pursuit of the material and spiritual needs of capitalist progress was of a kind which is unfamiliar to us today; but it was very real nonetheless. The march of progress in this supposedly laissez-faire era was assured by an almost incredible variety of intersecting collective structures, both private and public. For every one episode of mindless industriousness, such as the rapacious development of towns such as Coatbridge or Motherwell by iron magnates and engineers, there were two of regulation or collective effort. Even within industry, achievements such as the building of the Forth Bridge out of mild steel or the construction of the great steamships depended on a vast network of collective relationships. And the building of the everyday fabric of the nineteenth-century city was fuelled by a vast mosaic of initiatives of aspiration and trust. This ranged from the combined efforts of small speculators and public regulation agencies in house-building, to the grand municipal projects of public health, utility supply and slum clearance.

In the arrangement of the town as a whole, a new phase of planned settlement began, rejecting the old crammed burghs for new layouts. This age tried to bring order to the city above all through processes of separation, specialisation and sanitisation. Things that were old, muddled together, mixed, dense and dirty were to be ordered, segregated and made new. New and specialised public and private spheres of life coalesced. In this Utopian quest, with its powerful urge to the future, the drive to the future became stronger and stronger. The focal Edinburgh New Town street grid, with its axial monuments, was succeeded by the open Glasgow Blythswood grid. The chaos of modern society was offset by a vast effort of concerted urbanism, and the eighteenth and nineteenth centuries saw hundreds of planned towns, villages and suburbs. The Edinburgh, Aberdeen and Glasgow new towns pointed to a new pattern of segregation of public and private, a reduction of density, rejecting the old integrated, hierarchical patterns for a more decentralised type of elitism. They were, essentially, exclusive suburbs populated by freely cooperating individuals. In the planning of these suburbs, the initial pattern of rigid grids, contrasting strongly with the old dense towns and subjugating the landscape, was replaced from the early nineteenth century by a more flowing, irregular landscaped suburb type. And the scope of planned development was extended back into the old areas by an even bolder trend of

Moray Estate, Edinburgh

Woodlands Hill, Glasgow

planned reconstruction, a 'City Improvement' programme of massive surgery, which involved the carving of wide new roads through the existing decayed fabric.

In the architecture of individual buildings in this era, historic forms were still used to give authority, but these were drawn from a much wider range of sources; precise styles, or mixtures of them, were used to signify meaning. These included meanings which undermined previous orthodoxies; for example, 'national' styles asserted autonomy from the universal authority of antiquity. It is for this reason, this dynamic relationship of past and future, that we call this the 'Historicist Age'. Up to the early twentieth century, the ideals of modernity and progress were expressed in forms and concepts grounded in the past – whether the ideal cosmopolitan past of classical antiquity or the more immediate, emotive concept of the romantic national past.

This reconciliation of the old and the new in the styles of facades helped prevent the polarisations in society expressing themselves in polarisations within architecture. Its use of styles to denote specific values and purposes – otherwise known as 'eclecticism' – was used to unify, spatially, even the most discordant elements of nineteenth-century society. The monumental architectural and landscape ensemble of the Mound in Edinburgh, for instance, is dominated by setpiece buildings of the two opposing denominations of the great schism of the Disruption, along with a number of specialised secular monuments. These were composed into a whole by a single architect (W. H. Playfair). There were also incessant efforts to legitimise the new building types of modern society by adapting older patterns of a place-specfic character, whether topographic or geological. The long-standing Scots tradition of stone building was adjusted to the subtle gradations of eclecticism and the high finishes demanded by industrial society. Stone building was redefined from the old rough, mass walls to an industrially produced ashlar skin of monumental imagery. There was a special kind of sensuality of the severe masonry wall and the monumental town plan: the pursuit of extreme subtlety of shades of stone greyness culminated in the nineteenth-century building of 'Granite Aberdeen'.

More generally, in place of the old dispersed power centres of feudal society, a new, more concentrated topographical template of Scottish urban architecture began to emerge, dominated by urban values and by the bipolar east-west relationship of the Central Belt. As early as 1816, Walter Scott could contrast 'our metropolis of law, by which I mean Edinburgh' with 'our metropolis of mart and gain, whereby I insinuate Glasgow'.[4] One of the most remarkable achievements of this era was that it was able to sustain such varied interpretations of spiritual, past-rooted modernity at the same time – where today's Clone City has almost none at all. And this was no accidental, adventitious variety, but a careful enhancement of topographic and cultural patterns of difference, building especially on the growing contrast, in the post-1800 era of mass urbanisation, between the expansive, modernising west and the romantic, reflective east. That contrast is specially important because, in it, we begin to encounter for the first time a reaction against the architecture of progress and the very tentative beginnings of the concept of inclusive or cumulative modernity – the concept which forms the main theme of this book.

It was Glasgow, and the west, which addressed more directly the most thrusting, forceful aspects of the spirit of the age, with its capitalist Utopianism and elite freedoms. Here was a monumental industrial city fed directly by the pure water of the Highlands, energised by religious-capitalist zeal, and looking out across the ocean to America and the wider world. James Salmon caught the spirit of exultant progress when he told the Glasgow Architectural Society in 1858 that

in the providential development of our species, cities have become not only the marts of commerce, but of civilisation. The anvil of improvement, when struck aright in the heart of a great town, makes its vibrations felt in the remotest boundaries of a land . . . Let the morality of our cities be kept pure, and the potency of the example will elevate the righteousness of a whole people. Instruments of mighty power, the daily breathings of a great city vibrate through the pulses of a kingdom.[5]

Glasgow surged outwards in an unstoppable tide of new development, of open grids of tenements and flowing green villa suburbs, at the same time as it began radical surgery on its own heart, tearing down the old town completely with a ruthlessness which anticipated the redevelopments of the twentieth century. And it celebrated its glory by building itself a palatial headquarters in the 1880s, whose majestic modern classicism was clad in symbolic sculpture to exalt the city's global imperial mission.

The Glasgow ethos of spiritual entrepreneurship was celebrated above all in the work of Alexander Thomson. He argued that the monumental city had a calling higher and more enduring than ephemeral moneymaking:

the mark of the builder, above all others, stands up to mark the progress of successive generations – the well-defined links of a chain which seems calculated to bind the end to the beginning, and unite mankind into one family.[6]

The spiritual took precedence over the material: 'let us ever bear in mind that the business of commerce is inferior to the business of life.'[6] Glasgow was a theatre of the Scottish urban sublime, and even its greatest individual buildings fitted into that collective setting and open-ended process: Thomson insisted that 'insubordinate variety in architecture is a sure sign of want of culture.'[7] In his view, the experience of the monumental city by the citizen should be analogous to the experience of divine revelation, whether through scripture or through confrontation with the wilderness of nature:

an indescribable, strange consciousness, which every instant becomes more intense, that he is standing there alone, the only living thing before God . . . His terror melts into ecstatic joy; and, exulting in the love of God, he finds new strength and passes on his way.[7]

In parallel with Glasgow's classical modernity ran the growing strain of national romanticism, concerned more directly with the past and with the irrational. This at first stemmed from the conservatism of Edinburgh society, relative to Glasgow's. The planning of the first New Town remained quite hierarchical and enclosed by comparison with the Glasgow open grid. By the early nineteenth century, this somewhat reactive principle had become transformed into something positive and creative: a total vision of the city as a work of art, embracing all its built and landscape elements within a controlled network of vistas.

From the start, that control included a place for the Old Town, guaranteeing the existing and the old a special place within the framework of progress. That balance developed ideas that had already begun to emerge in the country estate planning of aristocratic 'improvers'. From the very beginning of the crusade to modernise and transform, one eye had always been cast backwards as well as one forwards, seeking to bed the new into the context of the old and of the natural landscape. Despite the fundamental cultural break of the Reformation, this was always a modernity with deep roots. The pioneering improvers of the early eighteenth century, such as Lord Mar or Sir John Clerk, tried to enlist the moral authority of antiquity and heritage by juxtaposing industrial projects with historical landscape gardening and imagery of family and national lineage. Later in the eighteenth century and early in the nineteenth, the idealisation of the Jacobites as symbols of a lost pre-Improvement past, the romantic cult of Ossian and the writings of Scott established the Scottish historical and myth-making consciousness as an indispensable counterpart to modernising revolution. That applied abroad as much as at home: Napoleon, after all, carried a copy of MacPherson's Ossian poems in his pocket on campaign.

By the mid- and late nineteenth century, the juxtaposition of romantic purity and modernity was found right across the country, for example in the ubiquitous 'Scotch Baronial' country houses with their modern plate-glass windows and domestic conveniences. But eventually the cult of Scottish tradition became especially associated with Romantic Edinburgh, in the novels of Robert Louis Stevenson, and it began to feel the influence of the growing pressures for social reform. The embrace of wild natural land-scape in the city, and the reconciliation of the old and the new towns, began to be interpreted as a metaphor for a wider social reconciliation. Whereas the New Town originally had been sharply demarcated from the Old, now both were embraced in a wider romantic vision of urban growth and renewal: a complex layering of successive modernities. The Old Town had undergone City Improvement Trust (CIT) redevelopments of a very different type to those of Glasgow, aiming to enhance rather than liquidate its historic fabric. The embrace of the old by the new was expressed literally in J. J. Burnet's 1886 Edinburgh International Exhibition complex, whose metal-and-glass Beaux-Arts structure contained, embedded within itself, a turreted reconstruction of the Old Town by Sydney Mitchell. We should bear in mind that it was at just this time that, overseas, some Scottish colonial engineers and imperial ideologists had begun to modify their old disregard for indigenous traditions in favour of concepts of coexistence, such as the 'dual mandate'.

THE MODERNIST AGE

The Historicist Age had devised an almost incredible variety of poetic ways to express the reconciliation of modern change with the legacy of the past, using historical forms as formulaic ways to balance freedom and order, image and use, and synthesising those solutions into powerfully monumental forms.

By the beginning of the twentieth century, however, many began to see its approach as fundamentally intolerable. Its balances depended on hierarchies and forces that were now starting to seem undemocratic and unsustainable in the twentieth century, especially after the huge casualties of World War I. As that century dawned, there were growing demands for national unity, and an end to the polarisations caused by capitalism. These were motivated, at first, not by opposition to imperialism, but by the reverse – by the urge to compete better. Arguably because of rising material standards and expectations, there was growing disquiet about the city: confrontations of social classes formed the domestic counterpart to the confrontations of nations and empires. Dickens in England had already attacked Coketown as a place of soulless worship of 'fact'. Now that critique became generalised across Europe, as critics in almost every country attacked the city as the scene of chaotic mass reproduction.

This was an accusation both of anarchy and of regimentation; of the wrong sort of freedom and the wrong sort of order. The Historicist Age had damned its predecessor as excessively hierarchical. Now it, in turn, was rejected for the same reason. Its built environments were seen as impossibly polarised between meanly utilitarian structures and prestige monuments bombastically loaded with ornament; and individual buildings were likewise seen as polarised between their fronts and their backs. The most attacked type of all was the working-class tenement, which was branded an anthill of promiscuous density, with a formal facade wallpapered across it. The precise, vast range of architectural styles, whose quality was assured by machine production, was now seen as a proliferation of meaningless variety, all the more debased for its machine production, and opposite in character to the 'real' past. Meaning in architecture now could be conveyed only by a general approach, an attitude of mind.

In many ways, the resemblances between the targets of those attacks and the environments of our Clone City today are startling. Both were dominated by the dislocations and polarisations of materialistic globalisation and disembedding. If the reformisms and ideals of the nineteenth century are of interest to us, then these critiques of their cloned debasement, and the solutions put forward, must be even more pertinent. Broadly speaking, there were two main groups of critiques and solutions: a complex critique

Gorgie, Edinburgh

Tanshall, Glenrothes New Town

put forward initially by the social and cultural reformist Patrick Geddes, and the outwardly more forceful solutions eventually adopted by the Modern Movement, especially after 1945. Although they seem at first glance very different, the two were linked quite closely, and we can learn much from them – so long as they are seen together.

In discussing Geddes's ideas, we need immediately to confront the danger of hailing him as a prophet whose ideas can be uncomplicatedly adopted today. In fact, part of his present-day charisma as a prophet figure stems from the fact that he was very much of his time, as the charismatic leader of a secular reform movement with overtones of a personal cult or sect. This contrasted sharply with the more disciplined, bureaucratised movements of the later era of fascism, but still had an authoritarian, elitist edge that is alien to us today – to say nothing of its overtones of eugenics and race.[8] Yet Geddes was responsible for a group of remarkable insights into the urban condition, which significantly carried forward the countermovement of inclusive rather than exclusive change. He developed it to the point where it could for the first time be called a coherent world view – a world view which would have some significant lessons for the later twentieth century. Here we need to make a second cautionary remark: that his views make sense to us, a century later, only when seen through the filter of what followed. There can be no question, for instance, of 'returning to Geddes' as a reaction against Modernism or Postmodernism.

Geddes blamed the regimented chaos of his age on uncontrolled industralisation, whose symbol of cloning was not electronic space but machine production. This, he argued, was a 'Palaeo-technic Age', whose disorder, echoing Stevenson's *The Strange Case of Dr Jekyll and Mr Hyde*, he attributed to its separation of the technology of material progress from any controlling human sensibility. This had forced the various elements of society, and the successive phases of human development, into unnecessary and destructive conflict. The Edinburgh New Town, for example, had been built at the expense of the Old Town; and the industrial class system had institutionalised a destructive contest over material redistribution. The architectural results were a polarisation between 'slum' and 'super-slum', the latter denoting the bumptiously jostling buildings of the ruling classes. Ominously, he predicted that the logical conclusion of that process of polarisation and confrontation would be world war.

The remedy Geddes advocated was a new kind of organic process, 'planning', to supersede the Palaeotechnic processes of conflict. There was to be a linked reconciliation of people, place and historical process. The divisive feuding of the classes over material goods would be replaced by a more unified, 'aristo-democratised' citizenry dedicated to the intensification of cultural excellence and the pursuit of an Aristotelian ideal of virtue. The fragmented spatial urban patterns of the Palaeotechnic city, a clone-like artefact divorced from context, would be replaced by the harmony of the 'Neotechnic' city, which he conceived either as a simple pyramidal model based on the Greek *polis* with its acropolis and rural hinterland, or as a more complex, yet still harmoniously coordinated agglomeration of cities for the modern industrial age: the 'conurbation'. One of the archetypes of the conurbation as a type, he argued, was the Central Belt of Scotland, which he dubbed 'Clydeforth'.

These cultural and spatial patterns were to be integrated into a new concept of urban history, which rejected the thrusting linear drive of Progress for a cyclical framework of ever renewing visions of the good life here and now. The aim would be not the ever receding vision of Utopia, but a realisable 'Eutopia': a doctrine of practical civic betterment grounded firmly in what already exists. This concept of cultural process Geddes conveyed most arrestingly in the *Arbor Saeculorum* (Tree of the Epochs), a diagram of open-ended cultural evolution which demonstrated

the two-fold aspects of each historic era, temporal on one side, spiritual on the other. The tree has its roots amid the fires of life, and is perpetually renewed from them; but the spirals of smoke which curl among its branches blind the thinkers and workers of each successive age to the thought and work of their predecessors.[9]

If we, in the present chapter of this book, are now engaged in an archaeological investigation into the layering of Utopias which forms the process of city evolution, it was Geddes who first explicitly suggested such an approach, in opposition to blindly driving, linear Progress.

Of the individual elements of the great Tree of the Epochs, the most solid and integral of all was the city itself. Its civic culture and materially enduring architecture acted as a kind of germ cell for constant renewal. Here Geddes developed not only the growing integrative conceptions of Old and New Edinburgh, but also the ideas of the pioneering Austrian city planner Camillo Sitte, who argued that architects of the modern city must before all else learn the spatial and psychic lessons of the existing city fabric – even if their own eventual designs look nothing like it! The *Arbor Saeculorum* held out a radical alternative to the aggressively modernising interpretation of progress. Everything that already existed was, potentially, of equal value for its contribution to the cumulative whole, and to its organic development in the future.

Geddes's vision of the city of the future, his doctrine of 'civics', was grounded in place – in the real city set in its cultural and landscape hinterland, the city in its region or the conurbation. And it was grounded in history. Taking Edinburgh as an exemplar, Geddes argued that the topography, the social and economic structure and the cultural heritage – in his words, Place, Work, Folk – could all be brought together in a formula of reform. This would be done not through Haussmann- or CIT-style mass redevelopment, which he branded 'civic ruin', but through a staged sequence, beginning with 'survey' (a way of ordering through the imagination, by constructing a psychic geography), followed by small-scale interventions of 'conservative surgery' to heal rents in the existing fabric, combined with a more ordered expansion of open suburban growth on the outskirts. The result, he claimed, would be a renascent capital girdled by garden suburbs, with free access to greenery and nature. The importance of the old fabric of the city core was symbolic rather than literal. Like the monuments of public religion in the Greek *polis*, it would serve as a focus of collective aspiration. Geddes was emphatically not a conservationist, but a passionate moderniser. As his own interventions in the Edinburgh Old Town showed, he would happily demolish or alter old buildings at will if they stood in the way of his wider cultural vision for the future. And within his conurbation vision, the reformed new industrial city had its role to play alongside the old centres. In the case of Clydeforth, for example, it was above all in Glasgow that 'the science of civics, and the science of industrial cities, is growing up'.[10] Geddes summed up his concept of the interrelationship of past and future as follows: 'to the baser spirits the Saga of their fathers is nought – as if it never was; to the narrower it is all, but ended; yet to others it is much, and in no wise closed!'[10]

Paradoxically, in view of Geddes's trumpeting of practical Eutopia in opposition to ideal Utopia, his ideas, in practice, were highly Utopian in the context of the early twentieth century. After all, to someone living in an overcrowded slum dwelling, the call for a new classless culture city would have seemed almost spectacularly beside the point. Only later, once those urgent material crises of Geddes's own day had been alleviated, could his ideas begin to seem more practically relevant. Geddes attacked state socialism as 'Tyrannopolis', comparing it to the ants and bees in its disregard for individual life. But the early twentieth century was an unfolding era of mass enfranchisement, and what was demanded was mass social provision governed by party politicians, professional groups and bureaucrats, not 'centres of life' and 'cloisters' directed by a theocratic elite.

The dominant concept of twentieth-century city development, the decisive response to the debased, clone-like environments of the Palaeotechnic city, was indeed to be 'planning', but planning of a different sort to that advocated by Geddes. During the early and mid-twentieth century, especially after 1945, the two-centuries-old commitment to material and social advancement, far from

Stirling University

Castlemilk, Glasgow

being abandoned, was reinvigorated by egalitarian socialism, which widened the scope of betterment from a middle-class elite to the whole national community. All was to be overseen, all was to be planned, by the new architect of economic and social life – the state. On the one hand, everyone was to have access to the conditions of the good life. This was an unheard-of emancipation. But on the other hand, that opportunity was to be accompanied and guaranteed by an unprecedented order and collective discipline.

Architecture transformed itself in step with these changes. The Modern Movement, adumbrated in Scotland in the 1930s and fully introduced after World War II, totally rejected historicism's formulaic evocations of the past and demanded a far more direct engagement with the future and with society in the mass. The nineteenth century's use of eclectic styles as language-like formulae to integrate the Vitruvian values of architecture now seemed absurdly inadequate. The nineteenth-century built legacy now seemed to be totally riven by hierarchy and division: between buildings thought worthy of treatment as architecture and those not; and within the 'architectural' buildings, between the building carcass and the stuck-on ornament. Modern architecture would claim everything within its scope, and would aspire to treat everything with equal care. In keeping with the new demand that architectural meaning should be expressed through more general, abstract qualities, the Vitruvian criteria were accentuated to an extreme degree, and were set loose in free combinations.

The combination that seemed, on the surface, to be dominant was that of Functionalism: a highly forceful development of the technical and social criteria in a way that almost seemed to absorb the visual. This was a hard-hitting linear logic of material Progress and mass standardisation. The crusades of provision or coordination in areas such as low-rent housing and national plan-ning were governed by ideals of standardised mass provision (Fordism) and managerial efficiency (Taylorism). Many Modern planning and housing texts were largely composed of Taylorist and Fordist rhetoric. Until the mid-1940s, Glasgow kept control over this modernising discourse, especially through the work of

Burnet's partner T. S. Tait, a key representative of the Glasgow Beaux-Arts rationalist tradition and a forthright advocate of building standardisation.

Of all phases of architecture, the Functionalist concept of design was arguably the most essentialist, the most integrated, the least tolerant of loose ends. It was also marked by an unprecedentedly strong faith in progress and the New: for the first time the New, as such, was polarised against the Old, the New almost became a guarantor of order. In the conception of the city as a whole, the scope of rejection had expanded from the old centres rejected by the nineteenth century, to the industrial city as a whole. This new scope was symbolised by the 'Glasgow problem', which, from the 1930s, became the constant dominating obsession of Scottish planners. Vastly stepping up the nineteenth century's formulae of suburbanisation and inner redevelopment, they demanded a huge two-pronged programme of building of New Towns and 'comprehensive redevelopment', involving mass population displacement and surgical onslaughts on city and country alike. The entire Clyde Valley region was to be 'strategically' reshaped, but in separate west and east sections rather than as Clydeforth. The 'Glasgow problem' was addressed through the Clyde Valley Regional Plan (1946), prepared chiefly by Patrick Abercrombie and beginning with the designation of East Kilbride in 1946, while the east and the Forth Valley had its own plan, drawn up by Frank Mears.

Through the boldly surgical redevelopments and the new planned towns, the industrial clutter of Glasgow was to be replaced by a clean, rectilinear order of the New. The fact that Glasgow's municipal politicians were bitterly opposed to the Clyde Valley Plan, and did everything they could to frustrate the grand strategy, including a counter-plan for completely self-contained redevelopment by City Engineer Robert Bruce, only fuelled the onslaught. The fact that the resistance was being steered from the Glasgow Municipal Buildings, in all its vastly encrusted eclectic magnificence, heightened the polarisation. In fact, however, the municipal countermeasures were very similar: large new settlements on the

Knightswood, Glasgow

Dennistoun, Glasgow

city outskirts, at first using an old-fashioned tenement form, but increasingly using tower blocks. It was the municipal people who were responsible for the most extreme mass housing solutions, including large-scale 'direct-labour' building. In the age of total war, the 'Glasgow problem' seemed in many ways like a Stalingrad of the Scottish planning movement.

But despite the vast scale of the building and planning campaigns, the unified front line of Functionalist order proved to be something of an illusion. Behind the facade of newness and tabula-rasa planning, everything was constantly in flux, in both the layout of the city and the design of the individual building. From the beginning, the elements of order and newness were being challenged and even undermined by complicating counter-elements of dissolution and oldness. Even at this apparent high point of the dynamic, confrontational approach to the built environment, the inclusive counter-framework was not totally absent. Its persistence was symbolised by the fact that after 1945, the leadership of the Scottish modern architecture and planning movement passed from Glasgow, and the mechanistic Beaux-Arts rhetoric of Tait, to Edinburgh, where Robert Matthew, son of the partner of Lorimer, assumed control. Matthew, steeped in the Edinburgh tradition of cumulative modernity, tried to put into practice some of Geddes's key demands in the very different context of the decades of 'total war'. On the one hand, he powerfully promoted the ideal of the public architect-planner, and Functionalist principles of solving social problems through architecture and regional planning; he was co-author of the Clyde Valley Plan with Abercrombie. But on the other hand, he was concerned to foster a 'national Scottish' modern architecture inspired by the 'vernacular'. The regional planners hailed Geddes as their prophet: they saw their solution as a Neotechnic response to the Palaeo-technic 'Glasgow problem'. And in the east, Geddes's son-in-law Frank Mears prepared an openly Geddesian regional plan, urging the enlargement of small towns. Within Edinburgh, Matthew's university colleague Percy Johnson-Marshall promoted a plan for the reconstruction of the university zone with an advanced decked layout, but justified it in terms of a Geddesian intensification of the inner city.

Architecturally, the most important complication of strict Functionalism was an architecture of pure aestheticism. Following ideas and language first devised in 1890s Germany, this acknowledged social and technical considerations, if at all, only through poetic metaphors. As early as the turn of century, the work of C. R. Mackintosh pioneered this type of modernity, by emphasising the unfettered, psychological freedom of the individual artist to express intense feeling and emotion, purged of moral or social baggage. Subsequent generations of Modern architects realised the potential of those ideas, even within the most traditional and hierarchical building types. For example, the work of Gillespie, Kidd & Coia developed the Mackintosh tradition of expressionistic freedom in a series of Roman Catholic church and educational buildings, culminating in the new St Peter's Seminary, Cardross (1959–66). In an influential series of public and residential buildings, the Borders architect Peter Womersley argued for an architecture of pure *uenustas*, an architecture as 'sculpture'.[11] And Basil Spence's work emphasised the primacy of appearance almost to the exclusion of all else. Significantly, Spence's early independent practice was dominated by the design of exhibition interiors.

In city planning, too, the order of the new was constantly offset by pervasive elements of freedom, symbolised by the word 'space'. 'Space' and 'form' were the two key terms of the new Modernist *uenustas*. Here we reach a fundamental dividing point, a point of departure not only for the 1940s–60s, but also for many of the constraints and opportunities which face us today. This was a sea change whose repercussions will constantly recur throughout this book. In the Historicist Age, urban space, however sweepingly or romantically conceived, was structured by fundamental hierarchies and inequalities. Under modernism, on the other hand, it was 'space' which symbolised the aspiration to do away with these barriers and constrictions.

The new, Modern concept of 'space' had, above all, the connotations of openness, freedom and internationalism. Physically, it was a completely fluid conception uniting the inside of the dwelling with the city as a whole within a single openness. Its three-dimensionality was symbolised above all else by the use of soaring multi-storey blocks to rupture the traditional horizontal city. At first, the freedom of planned space was seen in paradoxically disciplined terms, very different from the liberal nineteenth-century freedom symbolised by lines of separate spiky suburban villas. This was a freedom of the mass, a collective emancipation, which invoked the boldest elements of the Scottish tradition of planned order. In the aim of imposing built order on the landscape, not even the grandest landscaped patrician spaces of the eighteenth century could rival the insolent audacity of Cumbernauld Town Centre, a futuristic megastructure planted on an escarpment facing the foothills of the Highlands, or the Hutchesontown/Gorbals redevelopment in Glasgow, its layout of blocks flatly overriding the old closed-in street patterns. Modernist tower blocks tried to give a collective grandeur to the mass building of individual homes.

Yet even here, there was the germ of a revival of more individualistic concepts of space, tied especially to the growing emphasis on private mobility through the motor vehicle. As the climate of wartime discipline faded from memory in the 1950s and 1960s, replaced by an age of growing personal affluence and freedom, energetic attempts were made to devise new and more flexible concepts of planning. At Cumbernauld, a deliberately complex urban form was combined with an unprecedented level of provision for car ownership, including a complete grade-separated road network and separate pedestrian path system. It was often hailed, at the time, as a 'motor town', an 'ongoing laboratory of city-making' whose 'regionalite' inhabitants could aspire to an 'American' life of mobility.[12] As recently as 1945–6, Robert Bruce's grand Glasgow municipal plan had proposed a city-centre redevelopment of hierarchical, disciplined dignity, with rigid Beaux-Arts lines of skyscrapers, as had T. S. Tait's axial, monumental plan for the Glasgow 1938 Empire Exhibition. Cumbernauld's flexible plan, hardly more than a decade later than Bruce, seemed to belong to a different world. This was an open modernity for an increasingly open society. And these counter-trends of freedom were paralleled by another counter-trend, which built more straightforwardly on the Edinburgh and Geddes tradition to emphasise oldness and *genius loci*. At the same time as Glasgow's bulldozing redevelopments, other Scottish Modernist designers, especially those building on a smaller scale and in historic burghs, such as Wheeler & Sproson or Robert Hurd, tried to respond creatively to the existing heritage that surrounded them. The Saltire Society Awards for housing design provide a continuous record of these solutions.

THE POSTMODERN AGE

Despite these complicating factors and counter-trends, Modernism was still ultimately a Utopian movement of progress and rejection, and ultimately it fell victim in turn to the seemingly unstoppable dynamic of that process. From the 1960s and 1970s, Modernism became increasingly attacked and undermined, and was succeeded by the age of Postmodernity. Here, once again, we emphasise our use of the term 'Postmodern' in its wider, and still continuing, sense of a broad movement of culture, rather than in its narrower and now rejected usage as an architectural label: we will return in due course to discuss the significance of that rejection by architects.

In society at large, the Postmodern Age was a new era of renewed capitalist liberalism. It retained all its dependence on radical social and economic change, and its ability to corrode anything traditional in its way. But the most vital governing force, the simple crusading logic of linear progress, now disappeared. The new age began to turn its fire against the newly 'old' structures and communities of socialist discipline and collectivity – but the polemic was no longer tied to an onward-driving vision. During the 1980s in Scotland, out of resentment against Thatcherism, people for a time kept up an outward reverence to the ethos of social democracy. But eventually, the traditional

Dunbar

Cumbernauld New Town

ideals of social equity and wealth redistribution began to collapse in credibility. The old collective structures of authority – the state, the professions – were undermined and replaced by a new combination of social libertarianism and the order of the market. Intellectual authority also collapsed: the only framework that remained was Postmodern deconstruction, with its detachment of the signifier and signified, and its reduction of everything to layers of irony: everything became an image of everything else. The old 'grand narratives' such as historical progress or class struggle began to fade away, provoking a sense of relief and loss together.

Architecturally, the Postmodern era was initially dominated by reactions against Modernism. Once the latter had established total ascendancy after 1960, its manifestations had become increasingly extreme and prolific, with the exaggerated elements of chaos and order typical of the debased clone phase of any Utopian movement. At one extreme, the urban redevelopments of Functionalism involved tearing ever wider swathes of devastation across the city. And the tower blocks that were built on them increasingly seemed coarsely repetitive and utilitarian: the rationalistic ideas of mass production promoted in the 1930s by T. S. Tait were caricatured in the 1960s' mass cloning of Modernist flats by architects such as Sam Bunton or the contractors' company designers, with their package-deal designs. At the other, matching extreme, the modern architecture of unbridled poetic form began to experience its own problems, and was increasingly perceived as elitist and impractical. In response to these new polarisations, from the late 1960s to the 1990s, there began a spate of criticisms. Naturally, these took the form of complete reversals, as complete as the rejections of the Historicist by the Modernist Age. All the proudest boasts of Modernist designers began to be thrown back in their faces. Their central values were reversed: order became chaos, while the freedom of open space became alienation and oppression. In short, this was a new phase of cloning polemic.

In a reversal of the Utopian campaign against the tenements, Modernist towers now became the targets for deliberate demolition, and the tenement, loathed by all only a short time before, was transformed into a symbol of past harmony. The most symbolic of all these rejections was one which repudiated both poetic and tower-block Modernism in a single violent act: the dynamiting, in 1993, of the domineering concrete slab blocks designed by Spence three decades earlier as the centrepiece of the Gorbals redevelopment, blocks whose swaggering artistic freedom of design had come to be reviled, by those who lived there, as a brutal affront. During the explosion, in a final twist to the protracted saga, a flying piece of Spence's concrete crushed to death one of the local activists who had campaigned for the demolition.

For Modern architects, these reversals represented a catastrophic collapse of vocation. The old socialist ideal of the public architect subsided in prestige, leaving only a few redoubts such as the integrated design staffs of the New Towns. For architects, the 1970s and early 1980s were a generation of penance, following the collapse of a crusade that was now seen as a crime.

All the Modernist claims of comprehensive scope, of the integration of the Vitruvian qualities, now collapsed. Architecturally, there was a return to style, facades, decoration: Mackintosh became a hero and legitimising figure of this new stylism. The integrative claims of regional planning were equally rejected: the emptying out of the city and the building of new towns were attacked as a pernicious combination. In effect, where the Historicist Age had rejected the old burgh and the Modernist Age the industrial city, now it was the whole of the Modernist city, including its extensions and satellite new towns, that was rejected. In response to the 'failure' of the coordinating mechanisms of the Modernist city, there was a new fragmentation. The 'real city' was now identified as the nineteenth-century core, and the job of the planner as the repair of the damage inflicted on this core by Modernism; what lay outside would be left to its own devices, retaining the parcellising impulse of Modernism without its governing aspirations to comprehensiveness.

In the face of this withdrawal from Modernist ideals of coordination, the only ordering ideal at first tolerated was one which reacted strongly against Modernism: the conservation movement. We saw how the germs of the concept of an inclusive, cumulative city planning had developed since the eighteenth century as a counterpoint to modernity. Now, this concept was turned into the polemical weapon of another turn in the cycle of rejection: it became a simple reversal of Modernism's emphasis on the New. This was the first time that the Old and conservation had become directly involved within architectural polemical debate. That involvement was shaped, and encouraged, by a particular interpretation of conservation, stemming from the doctrines of the nineteenth-century English critic, William Morris. In accordance with a strictly linear view of historical progress, Morris insisted on a rigid separation of new buildings from old, and on the sacrosanctity of the latter. This was a concept of heritage which stemmed not from a love of modernity, but from a hatred of it: Morris detested the open, classical rationalism of the nineteenth-century Scottish city, and venerated instead the picturesqueness of English medieval villages.

But here there was a contradiction: if conservation was part of a wider collapse of credibility of linear material progress, and an element in the longer-term movement towards the cumulative and the inclusive, then a polemical, exclusive conservationism was a contradiction in terms. Geddes's view of the Edinburgh Old Town as an integral part of the *Arbor Saeculorum* – of heritage strictly serving the future – was continued by Robert Matthew, who saw nothing inconsistent, as a Modern architect, in founding a powerful committee to safeguard the future of the Edinburgh New Town. But in the wake of the crisis of Modernism, the Morrisian view of the heritage as inviolable was initially dominant. And there was an almost complete disappearance of belief in the active potential of architecture. For a number of years there was a broad presumption in favour of blanket conservation and against anything new. When people had to build new, then this had to be done as inconspicuously as possible. The most prestigious new monument of architecture – the Burrell Gallery in Glasgow – was one which effaced itself in a wood. The end of simple faith in linear

Progress, symbolised by the blowing up of tower blocks, seemed for the moment like the end of all faith in progress. For young architects coming into practice in the 1970s and early 1980s, the possibilities of architecture seemed to be limited to new tenement doors and back-court railings. More often than not, people just tiptoed between the broken glass.

When eventually, in the mid-1980s, a new phase of energetic, even frenzied, building succeeded the age of penance, the contradictions only grew. The values of Postmodernity had become dominant. Its reaction against Modernism was as much a change of ethos as of style, a revolt against state leadership and command planning. This movement, like all the others before it, had its initial ideals, and its subsequent debasements. Its combination of user participation and capitalist initiative seemed at first to be a powerful liberation and democratisation. There was a widespread public hunger for more brightness, decoration, variety and enclosed planning in the city, as a relief from the monumental greyness, openness and newness of much Modernist architecture. The drive for freedom had always been a central element of modern society. Now, in the revolt against massed discipline, the demand for individualism reached a new climax. But many of the resulting projects went to an extreme of small-scale parcellisation and gaudy brickwork, and mingled images of oldness and 'tradition' with modern functions in a licentious way – what is now labelled the 'Postmodernist style' of architecture.

The sheer panache of this architectural Postmodernism at its best was expressed in polarised eastern and western extremes: among Edinburgh designers, by Ian Begg's scenographic baronial outcrops; and among Glaswegians, by Gillespie, Kidd & Coia's late work, which combined a continuing spatial verve with profuse, Mackintosh-based decoration. The Mackintosh Revival's combination of commercial populism and architectural dynasty-building reached its climax in the 'Art Lover's House', a heritage centre constructed in 1989–96 in Glasgow on the basis of a famous set of competition drawings by Mackintosh. The building also houses a conference centre and the postgraduate department of the city's School of Art, complete with one of the world's most advanced holography-based design computers, supplied by the Ford Motor Company. The Art Lover's House is a microcosm of all the most disorientating elements of postmodernity, with its comprehensive separation of signifier and signified. Looking at this building, we have no idea what it is or what it represents: is it art or commerce, new or old, true or false?

Between these two gestural extremes of Postmodernist imagery, straightforward modern architecture seemed to have been squeezed out. And then, just as in previous architectural phases, the Postmodern vision passed on to its debased stage – in its case, the commodified and fragmented image environments of Clone City. The only difference from the past is, now, that the cycle has been speeded up. But precisely because of this telescoping, Clone City's vehement rejections of Modernist certainties are combined with much practical, behind-the-scenes continuity with Modernism. There is no simple break any more, no linear progression from the one 'movement' to the next. Clone City's anarchic mass reproduction of 'standards' and individual city elements is a banal perversion of Functionalism and Fordism, emptied of poetry and social idealism and hitched instead to a manic pursuit of computer-assisted variety. The Modernist characteristics of universal spreading parcellisation have been preserved, but turned into a polarised and fragmented form, dressed up by fundamentalist images: the centre as the 'traditional dense city', the suburbs as villages. The modern society of strangers, of civil indifference policed by the state, is concealed by the mask of 'traditional public realm'. The new private intimacy is concealed by the mask of urban-village community. Some of Modernism's most extreme elements of heroic form and banal functionalism are mixed together. Image and production are now mingled: everything is both 'designed' and for the 'market', and even the most banal speculative house has its own 'image'.

But the process of fragmentation and dissolution has gone even further. Postmodernity's rejection of grand narratives has undermined the viability of the polemical tradition itself, leaving

us in a state of compounded perplexity. Where previous generations could respond to alienation with calls for a new clarity,
homogeneity and essentialism, we today are in a state of paralysis,
unable to reach any consistent view of, let alone any vision for,
the present-day city.

During the 1990s, many architects have responded to this
impasse by reviving the forms of the Modern Movement, while
leaving unchallenged the cultural and economic context of postmodernity. The cleverest attempts have been made in the Netherlands, where neo-capitalist economics have been combined with
architectural images of social cohesion – trying to revive the poetic
and artistic aspects of Modernism, without its state paternalism
and materialism. In Scotland, this change from simple stylistic
Postmodernism to a more subtly postmodern Retro-Modernism
can be gauged most accurately by recent adjustments to the cult of
Mackintosh. Now he is hailed less as a source of PoMo decorative
vocabulary than as the founder of a dynasty of heroic form-givers,
stretching through to the Glasgow architectural practices and
schools of the present day. What has not changed, however, is
the underlying preoccupation with images, and the driving
impetus of the marketplace. The stuck-on decorations of the 1980s
have been succeeded by the gestural forms and spaces of today.
In 1994, for example, the then head of the 'Mac School', Andrew
MacMillan, lambasted Postmodernist Glasgow for its failure to
keep up with the global competition of culture cities and signature
architects: he challenged 'anyone to name one building built in
the last fifteen years in this city which is better than good third
rate. Which building could I show Enric Miralles?'[13] In a way,
these ideas represent a convergence by Europe with the concept
of Modernism that prevailed from the beginning in the United
States – as a lifestyle image, rather than a reformist ethos. We
should remember that Charles Jencks's definition of the 'radical
eclecticism' of the Postmodernist movement included 'Modernism'
as one stylistic option among others. And some Modern Movement
architects, such as Basil Spence – who tended to work from perspective to plan, rather than the other way round – already

anticipated this style-led approach. Unsurprisingly, it is they who have joined Mackintosh in the new pantheon of Retro-Modernism, a pantheon from which more complex and self-effacing Modernists such as Matthew or Alan Reiach, who left an active ideological and organisational legacy behind them, are excluded.

Thus the style and the label may have changed from Post-modernist to Modernist, but the context, of society and patronage, has not. Architecture is just as much responsive to the ruling power as ever, and that power today resides in the unbridled global market. Postmodernist architecture as a label, and Post-modernist styles, may have been rejected, but we are still stranded in the cultural context of rampant postmodernity. A 1997 instal-lation by artist Nathan Coley highlighted this predicament, juxtaposing a high-flown description of a Modernist icon, Le Corbusier's Villa Savoye, with pictures of a brick speculative showhouse, in order to suggest the mutually parasitical relation-ship of the architecture of heroic Retro-Modernism and the everyday environment of materialistic banality. The only possible escape from this vicious circle, the only way out of postmodernity's hall of mirrors and images, is to address the real issues of the built environment in which we all live – just as the real Modernists, such as Matthew, tried to do in their own day and in their own way.

A MONUMENTAL HISTORY: THE MODERNITY OF HERITAGE

> The manifold and tangled elements of Heritage and Burden from the Past.[14]

Our 'archaeological dig' on the site of Clone City has, as one would expect, produced no easy answers to our predicament, but a num-ber of fragmentary clues. The first of these clues is the realisation that Clone City forms part of a process that has spanned several centuries, a process of urban and architectural evolution through violent ruptures and about-turns towards Utopian opposites.

This framework has channelled the effects of economic and social change into its own powerful structure and conventions. In its time, it was a powerful stimulus to creativity and diversity. And even today, it still offers a deceptively uncomplicated way forward: all we need to do, it suggests, is to attack Clone City in the time-honoured way. To do so would be very easy: for example, potential criticisms of the emptiness of electronic space are little different from late-nineteenth-century criticisms of the alienating effects of machine production, or the 1970s critiques of empty Modernist space. But to do that would be to evade the issue. This is the second of the insights stimulated by our 'archaeological dig'. For the entire cyclical process is now increasingly exhausted and laden with fundamental contradictions; it cannot just carry on as normal.

The most important of these contradictions is the fact that the collapse in the belief in simple material Progress has undermined the viability of a simple cycle of rejections. Each Utopia had been formed on the ruins of the previous one. Latterly, these Utopias had become more rootlessly extreme – the all-new of Modernism, the all-old of conservationism. Since then, the collapse of teleological Progress has removed the dynamic, thrusting relation of past and future and the intense social-moral authority which gave each new Utopia its driving force. Now we find ourselves with nothing of substance out of which to build another authoritative 180-degree rejection, nothing from which we can construct any new Utopias. To try to build a Utopia out of old buildings or Postmodern images is a contradiction in terms. This we can clearly see, for example, in the case of today's Modernist Revival, a revival less like the old, passionate Utopias of the city than one of the cyclical style revivals of pop culture, and likely to last no longer than the latter.

We have to finally accept that we cannot simply escape from the dissolving forces of today's Postmodern globalism by constructing some new Utopian grand narrative. But this can be a liberating realisation, pointing us away from the Utopian cycle altogether, towards a new kind of critical narrative which will allow us to reform, not repudiate, Clone City and its problems. And the exhaustion of the dynamic of confrontation leads us inexorably to ideas reminiscent of Geddes's concepts of the *Arbor Saeculorum* and of cumulative or cyclical progress, Eutopia rather than Utopia.

The focus of any move towards reconciliation must be the still highly polarised forces involved in the most recent cycle of debates, since the 1960s. The missing branches of the *Arbor Saeculorum* are the newest ones: the still problematised Modern Movement, and the newly problematised Postmodernism. Thus our revisit of the ideas of Geddes must, paradoxically, involve rejecting any simplistic idea of a 'return to Geddes'. We can build on Geddes only if we also learn from the way in which his partial legacy was developed – however imperfectly – by his Modernist and Postmodern successors.

It is still only thirty years since the decline of the Modern Movement began in earnest, and our own attitudes to it are a tangle of disjunctions and continuities. The Modernist urban legacy still provides the banal, everyday materiality and the certainties around which or against which Postmodern spaces and forms have been constructed. Postmodern urban culture adopted from the conservation movement the sharp Morrisian polarisation between old and new, and applied it to the relationship between pre-Modernist ('good') and Modernist ('bad') urbanism. This equation is now neatly reversed by some Edinburgh advocates of the new Retro-Modernism, who equally mischievously attack heritage as the enemy of good new architecture – and so on, potentially *ad infinitum*. Geddes pointed to the destructive implications of this polarised framework, which in all cases segregates heritage from architecture, relegating it to theme park status.[15]

Within a cumulative, rather than confrontational framework of logic, the recent heritage is in many ways the most relevant. And indeed, while the Modern Movement's driving total logic of Utopian order is unacceptable to us today, this was also a period which powerfully and comprehensively tried to address the aim of freedom – social and spatial – in our cities. In particular, the later Modernism of the 1960s, alongside all its now obsolete rhetoric of limitless materialism, pointed to numerous concepts of flexibility and individuality that are central to our existence today; for example, the demand for personal mobility still continues to grow even now, despite the mounting controversy over the respective roles of private and public transport in achieving it. It is a basic constraint on all the attempts to recover order, collectivity and justice in the city today, that if these attempts ignore today's demand for freedom of choice, then they amount to nothing more than rhetoric. What we now must do is to look again at the Modern Movement concept of ordered openness, so that we can learn from its mistakes – and their successes.

Ironically, it is not contemporary architects, but the activists of the heritage movement, such as the Scottish branch of the internationalist organisation DOCOMOMO, who are forcing the pace in the re-evaluation of the Modern Movement today. Where architects are in many cases preoccupied with the heroic-artist strand of Modernism, in other words with an essentially postmodern image concept, the heritage movement is pioneering a broader appraisal of the entire Modernist built environment, with its overarching ideals of emancipatory building for all, and assessing its potential lessons for us today. At DOCOMOMO's fifth annual conference in Stockholm in 1998, dedicated to the social ideals of Modernism, chairman Hubert-Jan Henket identified today's laissez-faire nihilism as a reaction against the dirigisme of the Modernist Age, and issued a clarion call for a new phase of social modernity which would learn from those mistakes: 'democracy is still worth fighting for. An emancipated society is still worth fighting for. We know now we can't simply build the future, but we can help shape it!'

How can we reconcile this wider modern heritage with our needs today, so that we can resume the narrative of progress in a new way, no longer driven forward but carrying our past along with us? That question will repeatedly recur throughout the remainder of this book. The process of reconciliation has to encompass both people and place. In the former case, it has to draw on the twentieth-century lessons of social commitment and planning by the state, while leaving behind the twentieth century's confrontational urban politics of class and mass ideology for new democratic and participatory ideals. And in the latter case, it has to reconcile the modern demand for free-flowing form with the authority of the city of cumulative narrative, and apply the same principles to the new space of the dispersed conurbation. The conurbation, in its present-day form of commodified chaos, is unsustainable. But we cannot simply avoid the issue by doing away with it altogether. We have to work within it, modifying and reforming and re-embedding the legacy of Modernism and Postmodernism; for example, by combining the lessons of Modernist regional planning for the Central Belt as a whole with the more deeply rooted cultural characteristics of west and east.

With the recovery of the whole narrative of our architectural heritage, and the reconnection of past and future, the relationship of architecture to cultural identity and the democratic process can begin to be redefined in dynamic and liberating terms. Freed from hole-in-corner preservationism, we can hope for a true victory of the cumulative city, the city as a narrative paradigm, the city as a realisation in stone of the Geddesian *Arbor Saeculorum*. For the narrative to retain its power, the processes of renewal must continue. Nietzsche argued that there are two strands of history, the antiquarian and the monumental: the first concerned with the past for its own sake, the second with the past as an inspiration to the future. The history of the modern Scottish city is in that sense, as well as literally, a monumental history. The central issues of modernity have not gone away. We are still faced with the confrontations of progress and history, and of order and freedom, and the demand to regulate change by forethought and planning. And the dilemmas they pose have grown even more complex.

Even if we wanted to, it would be impossible to return to some kind of unsullied, unmodern tradition, because Scottish architectural history and tradition have been shaped by three centuries of modernity and openness. Yet it is equally impossible to return to the now discredited diktats and expert prescriptions of the mid-twentieth-century era of mass building: a self-conscious modern stylistic revival can only be ephemeral. The only way out is forward, towards freedom; yet to proceed at all, we must carry our past along with us. For Geddes, seeking to plan the culture city of the twentieth century, the 'manifold and tangled elements of Heritage and Burden from the Past'[14] were the inescapable springboard for that future – a future in which the material fabric of the city would play a uniquely important role, by simultaneously stabilising society and inspiring it to fresh efforts of freedom and renewal. For Robert Matthew, too, the Modern Movement had to be rooted in people and place. But neither Geddes nor Matthew could decisively break out of the cycle of violent rejections. Can we succeed in doing so today, after a further century of Utopian turmoil?

To stand any chance of achieving our aim, we have to embark on the two strands of renewal together: the renewal of people and the renewal of place. The challenge of place is a long-term task of restoring integrity both to the ideal Scottish city and conurbation, and to the real conurbation of Clydeforth, in its cultural and landscape settings. But before that and all else, there is the challenge of people: the burning need to recreate committed citizens out of Clone City's market atoms, to reintegrate everyone in our society with the process of building the democratic city.

Parliament Square, Edinburgh

Wyndford, Glasgow

3
BUILDING A DEMOCRACY
A Reconciliation of People

Where there is no vision, the people cast off restraint; but blessed are they who keep the law.[16]

Reflect every day, reflect well on the greatness of our beloved city. And remember that greatness did not simply happen of its own accord. It was built up by past generations of Athenians – by citizens with bold aspirations, citizens inspired by duty, citizens committed to excellence.[17]

If we are seeking a new formula of order with freedom in the built environment, a formula which reconciles and builds on the multi-layered lessons of the past, we have to start not with buildings, but with people. And here it is necessary to return in more detail to the relationship of architecture and democracy now and in the past. We have to focus on two contrasting interpretations of that relationship: representation and participation. Or, put more simply: the architecture of democracy and the democracy of architecture.

During the Historicist Age, the growing freedoms of the many, in a time of unprecedented wealth, were supported by a system which perpetuated gross inequalities. Accordingly, the relationship of architecture to democratic ideals was highly selective, in terms of both representation and participation, and was firmly contained within the hierarchy of architectural decorum. For example, the municipal democracy enjoyed by the merchant classes was embodied in the building, and celebrated in the sculpture, of lavish town halls, while buildings for the lower classes were far more modest in scale and symbolism.

In the Modernist Age, architecture remained just as much as

ever an inherently disciplining medium, just as much a medium within which vast power and resources were inevitably at stake – but for the first time people sensed the possibility of a major redistribution of that power. Responding to the development of mass politics, the representational role of architecture was flung wide open and the old hierarchies were levelled, with austere yet spatially flowing forms applied to all building types alike. And much more importantly, there were real attempts to create a mass participatory architecture, an architecture not just symbolising but involving all the people. Everyone, not just an elite, had the right to good architecture. For Modernism's Functionalist strand, the very essence of their creed was to build for all. Robert Matthew argued in 1952 that the only worthy comparison was Periclean Athens: 'for the first time since the fifth century BC, public architecture has become popular architecture – in the strict sense, by the people, for the people.'[18]

The Modern Movement's most burning aspirations were concentrated in its most everyday programmes and above all in that of mass housing. The aim of providing self-contained dwellings for all, through social agencies rather than the hated landlords, was seen in messianic terms of emancipation – and this applied equally to the programmes driven by the planning experts and by the municipal housing crusaders. In the words of Edinburgh Labour councillor Pat Rogan, 'it was a magnificent thing to watch, as I did many times, whole streets of slum tenements being demolished – all those decades of human misery and degradation just vanishing into dust and rubble!'[19] And for his Glasgow counterpart, Housing Committee convener David Gibson, there could be no more satisfying way of spending a spare evening than to drive round newly completed tower blocks, gazing at the lights shining out from 'all the families translated from gloom into happiness'.[19]

But, just as the radical democracy of Athens was ultimately undermined by its own instabilities, so equally the Modernist Age's formula of mass participation was dependent on a variety of mechanisms that proved mutually conflicting. Ultimately the strongest trend was the way in which its provision of self-contained dwellings and other personal social services encouraged a more and more individualised urban society. This undermined its own key ordering mechanisms, notably its reliance on ideologies of mass solidarity and exclusion (whether of classes or of whole nations), and its dependence on authoritarian command structures and mechanistic formulae, which treated 'the people' as passive consumers of material goods. We need to remember that there was no political conflict over this question. In the early to mid-twentieth century, both capitalism and socialism prided themselves on making material goods widely available throughout society. And although Modernism introduced to architecture for the first time the concept of the use and users of buildings, it defined the user as not a real but a theoretical person, whose needs were to be scientifically discovered and provided for by the architect expert and the state. Such a definition could not long be sustained.

When, as we saw in the last chapter, these contradictions burst into the open from the 1960s, and the triumphant ascendancy of Modernism came to an end, the result was not the disappearance of conflicts and structures of domination and material accumulation, but their incorporation in a postmodern field of commodification and images. For example, there are prolific images and slogans of post-1968 people power, especially through the mechanisms of participatory involvement, nostalgic community and consumer conservatism. Where Modernism made a direct attempt to realise its ideals of disciplined mass participation, using the massive exercise of power and direct provision by the state in its various competing agencies, in today's Clone City the exercise of power, and the pressure for materialistic advancement, have hidden themselves behind layers of images. The confrontation of producers and consumers has been maintained, but changed into a laissez-faire capitalist rather than state dirigiste form. Power is still there – it must always be somewhere, in the patronage of architecture – but it can no longer be controlled or even properly identified. In place of the old professional or elected authority figures, there are now the secret commercial deal-makers, such as the local-authority development promoters, or those, such as Prince Charles, who make demagogic appeals direct to 'the people'.

In Clone City, images of democratic participation and representation serve as cloaks for materialist accumulation. Here the most prized democratic mechanism, 'choice', is defined not as the finding of an ideal or a way of life but the selection of objects and commodities. This is no more than a choice between stuck-on standard elevations; between parliament images fuelled by the freedoms of computer-aided design; between communities shaped by the pre-structured choice of kerbside appeal, to be picked off the shelf like cereal packets; and ultimately, between rival cities, their local authorities transformed from planner-guarantors of social reconstruction to bitterly competing development companies. If Modernism only partially realised the representational and participatory ideals of a democratic architecture, in Clone City both are reduced to a cloak for the vested interests of the marketplace. If Robert Matthew's Periclean vision of authority-led democracy proved unsustainable in the face of social change, the cut-throat society that has followed it is likely to prove even more ephemeral. We would do well to remember what happened to post-Periclean Athens when it fell into the hands of demagogues: it was ruined by their sophistry, bribery and schemes of domination.

RETURN OF THE PROPHETS

Is there any way of escaping from this pervasive commodification of the social relations of city-building? To return to the dead end of pugilistic Utopianism, to the city as a battlefield, is no answer. The only possibility lies in the far more slow and painstaking task of trying to reform rather than repudiate Clone City, through positive rather than destructive means, building on what already exists. We have to carefully modify today's distorted relations between the producers and consumers of the environment, including a revitalisation of the role of the state. After all, our

Seafield Colliery, Kirkcaldy

Linlithgow Palace

position is not an entirely gloomy one. With the passing into history of the certainties of the Modernist Age, we are confronted not only with threats but with opportunities. In the wake of this decomposition, a new, creative aspect of globalisation is emerging from within, one which can exploit international links to fight the rule of blind competition, and create new collective identities of integrity and justice to combat mindless material accumulation. The social and cultural revolution that destroyed the old-style modernity of driving Progress is still under way, and its next targets are the blind rapacity and technology worship of postmodern capitalism: the values that represent the dark side of Clone City.

The key battleground of this movement is the still shifting balance between freedom and order in the definitions of identity, a process symbolised in the competing interpretations of the word 'choice'. All too aggressively obvious today is choice in its narrow and materialistic sense, a choice between objects and lifestyles in the unfettered market, invariably at someone else's expense. But emerging alongside it is a different kind of choice, of a way of life, of values, of identity. For with the collapse of the old, compulsory communities of the nineteenth and twentieth centuries – family, occupation, class, unitary nation – there is now no longer any essential, exclusive or compulsory identity. Collective aims must be pursued voluntarily, by individuals, and through ethical or aesthetic ideals rather than cognitive mechanisms. We cannot even rely for guidance any more on universalist discourse or intellectual authority. All experts are lay people in all fields other than their own narrow specialisms, and all individuals can now aspire to make intellectually informed choices and take greater responsibility for themselves.

Intimacy by choice; tradition by choice; identity by choice. This is a completely new phase in the modern search for openness and freedom, and something which contrasts but also connects with both the twentieth-century mass communities, and the nineteenth-century era of laissez-faire. This is potentially a global liberation, for the many rather than just for an elite. The collapse of the 'fortress nation', for example, opens up the possibility of enriching one's own roots by affiliating to many communities rather than just one nation, or of joining with people from other countries to solve common problems. Within the field of city planning, for example, the *Europan* movement embraces many thousands of participants in its initiatives of urban regeneration. With the growing implausibility and impracticability of simplistic national or international triumphalism, the need for a more diverse framework of identity, in the built environment as in other cultural arenas, is stronger than ever.

This withering away of coercive definitions of identity is paralleled by the decline of all formulae of materialistic salvation in the future, whether socialist or capitalist. Although this forms part of the more general decline of legitimacy of ideologies of materialist Progress, a more particular cause has been the nineteenth and twentieth centuries' very success in their crusades of social hygiene against the vast problems of disease and slums, a success which culminated in the great postwar housing drive. Consequently, those problems have been reduced to manageable islands, or redefined in strictly relative terms of inequality. For example, only 1 per cent of Scottish dwellings now fall within the 'below tolerable standard' criteria used to condemn the slums of the past. Some of these problems are still urgent ones: damp homes across the country contribute to epidemics of bronchial disease and asthma. Yet increasingly the definitions of inequality and injustice are moving away from areas of conventional material welfare into less easily quantifiable fields such as access to information and control of environment.

Clone City refuses to recognise this shift away from simple materialism: it denounces the 'failure' of welfare socialism but proudly puts in its place marketing images of even greater crudity. We, on the other hand, can recognise that socialist collectivism was highly effective in facilitating choices of identity in its own day. And we can modestly aspire to do even better – through very different means! The challenge of today is the same as it has ever been in the modern world: to stabilise the fundamental impulse of freedom and individuality through collective ideals. But that relationship now has to be reformulated to take account of the collapse of the authority of materialistic Progress.

That reformulation can be a confusing process at first, its early stages of decomposition and repudiation dominated by destructive clashes between conflicting individualisms and communalisms. For example, much of the initial critical response in Scotland to the disintegration of the ethos of state socialism has been pervaded by a kind of caustic nihilism. This replaced a gritty urban realism, which itself had earlier superseded the old interwar nationalist ideal of rural Scottish wholeness. Among many writers and artists, the only references to issues of cultural and social identity are metaphorical or highly indirect. Eventually, however, new concepts of democratic order can begin to emerge, responding to the decline of Progress by emphasising once more the stabilising authority of the past. The key differences are over how far that authority should be carried. Some react to the alienating effects of globalist systems by means of a 'fundamentalism' which advocates the revival of traditional coercive structures, laws of gravity or essential identities – at the risk of a lack of credibility through bombast, and a distorting idealisation of the past. Others more wholeheartedly embrace a continuing modernity, and try to offset the fragmenting character of globalist change through voluntary and pluralistic initiatives.

These new values of the post-Utopian age are debated using concepts and methods alien to conventional twentieth-century social-democratic politics and administration. With the scaling down of simple problem-solving materialism, attention begins to turn to the critical power of ideas, to visions stemming either from the formerly private realm or from the older moral-poetic-rhetorical tradition of public discourse. With the discrediting of straightforward equations between intellectual prescriptions and social reality, poetry and prophesy can present issues in heightened or distanced form. Rhetoric can be a way of highlighting injustice, even if we retain scepticism about its practical efficacy. And new ways open up of combating the Postmodern split between image and reality by reintegrating the two: for example, by visualising architecture, under all its Vitruvian headings together, as a kind of poetry in its own right.

Once we move beyond the initial stage of decomposition and disembedding, once we begin to move beyond the internally referential in search of moral fixity, we can begin to tackle broader questions of existence and identity. There we find a new diversity, previously unknown in this totalitarian century. The real potential of openness in modernity is revealed, and the optimistic, creative side of globalisation begins to unfold in a far more diverse variety of kinds of advocacy, ranging from detached, pluralistic commentary to passionate engagement. What seems to be opening up instead is a completely new vision of freedom with order, a new concept of modern identity within history. History is still the factor that structures and gives order to the drive for freedom and change. But whereas previously that historical order was driven on by the compulsion of the future, now the relationship between past, present and future is no longer a simple linear one but cumulative or even cyclical. The way forward to the future still beckons, but now in the form of an open-ended narrative. Now we choose when, where and how we proceed, and we carry our past always with us, adding to it as we go.

The withering away of authoritarian mass democracy allows older and more enduring values of social engagement to re-emerge. Can the frameworks of religion, for instance, help us help to find our way in the trackless desert of the global market? Here we find a spiritually based concept of hope for the future which contrasts with the ephemeral urgency of Utopian secularism, and which is combined, today, with a growing openness to social reality. Within the Roman Catholic Church, for example, the reforms inaugurated by the Second Vatican Council in the 1960s dramatically threw open the windows of the Church to the wider world – although this revolution is still, arguably, only half completed. And within the Church of Scotland, the kind of initiative of social commitment and ecumenism that was once on the margins – as in the work of the Iona Community since the 1930s and the 1950s–60s tenants' rights activism of Rev. Geoff Shaw's

Gorbals Group – has now moved to the centre. In the view of Richard Holloway, head of the Scottish Episcopal Church, all absolute moral systems and fundamentalisms constitute idolatry: God is a rock, but a spiritual rock that follows us, rather than standing still.

If religion has been secularised into a matter of personal choice and commitment, so, conversely, it is open to individuals to choose to 'sacralise' contemporary secular life, contemporary life in the city, by turning to a search for reality and integrity behind the fleeting images of the globalised marketplace. To Holloway, for example, some secular activities such as art and music can be priestly, precisely because they can overcome the postmodern split of image and reality: 'they don't just describe, or signify. They *"are"*. They become what they describe.' Beauty is 'an intrinsic and not an instrumental good – it's good in itself rather than good "for" something else.'[20]

A range of secular commentators and prophets have begun to contest today's blind materialism with ideologies of ethical revitalisation, many loosely bound up with the green movement's arguments concerning the interdependence of the human and natural worlds. Several contemporary Scottish philosophers, for instance, have cautiously laid down signposts towards a good life which respects our new freedoms, steering a path between the extremes of moral fundamentalism and nihilistic 'emotivism'. Alasdair MacIntyre proposes an external goal grounded in Aristotelian 'virtue', a voluntarily undertaken way of life which is good in its own right, rather than in its relation to any specific moral duties or practical tasks.[21] Individual and community both gain coherence and dignity by joining in that search, as, to overcome market atomisation, each individual has to strive for the good life in parallel with the wider evolution of social identity, in groupings such as family, nation or ideological community. The artists and poets, too, have taken up the challenge. The poet Ian Hamilton Finlay highlights the extremes of our dilemma in a detached, almost stoic critique which does not so much sacralise secular life as point to the possibility of doing so. Drawing on the

Postmodern revival of rhetoric, he argues that we have artificially segregated the religious from the everyday or secular – elements which he claims were seamlessly fused in the classical world. As a result of this division, the driving motors of modernity – the twin forces of freedom and order – have been allowed to develop free from any controlling spiritual sensibility: Finlay laments the 'unbuilt temples' of democracy.[22] Many younger artists demand a more direct engagement with the problems and communities of the city. The Environmental Art department at Glasgow School of Art, founded in 1985 by David Harding, has promoted the cause of art as a process in the city rather than an elite activity in galleries – a process which has had to combine a critical social stance with respect for people and topography, and to constantly renegotiate that combination. And likewise the militant neo-classical sculptor Alexander Stoddart insists that the chief significance of statuary is that of 'moral punctuation of the city'. It is rarely noticed, but 'without it, the sentence falls apart'.[23]

In any attempt to reintegrate image and reality in the modern city, architecture must occupy a central place. If music and poetry can be priestly activities, and the beauty of art can be an intrinsic good, in architecture the opportunity for direct experience is even more pervasive: we exist in it, live in it, work in it. And that experience is not purely aesthetic, but far more complex: as Vitruvius showed, architecture must also be practically useful and solidly built. The Vitruvian triad of *utilitas, firmitas, uenustas* is, in its own right, almost like a formula of performance art, applied to the whole city over centuries. The Scottish city itself can be, and at times in the past has been, an authoritative physical testimony of social and cultural change. While earlier periods' formulae of urban order are not literally applicable to us, owing to their inequality or authoritarianism, what can inspire us today is their material legacy. This is a heritage which we can appropriate as part of our own identity, simply by the fact that we live in it and use it daily. By its very presence and its accumulated authority, the built fabric of the city fulfils every demand for gravity and order. Yet by the fact that, as a narrative, it must by definition

Stirling Castle

St James Centre, Edinburgh

continue into the future, it can also enshrine freedom. The Scottish city is a monument to the open-endedness of modernity, a monument whose sheer scale and pervasiveness within society can help guide us towards an ordered vision of change – so long as we constantly reimagine and reinvigorate it. What now has to be put behind us is the idea that we can any longer relate to this complex heritage through the logic of fighting and confrontation.

This is a fundamental revision of the old dynamic logic of the architecture of crusading Progress, whether in its historicist or Modern Movement phases. It combines the necessity of a narrative to progress into the future with the central role of the past as a cumulative heritage to that future. That is the only sure way to fight the anarchy of Clone City. The very dissolution of the great, centuries-long crusade of striving opens up the prospect of its fulfilment. Ceasing to strain forward towards an ever distant City on the Hill, we look around us and realise that we are there already. The sum total of what exists now, in both its materiality and its psychic and sensual qualities, can be a springboard for a calmer and more inclusive concept of architectural history – for a second and more stable phase of modernity, which embraces the built legacy of its restless predecessors as part of itself. Then, in turn, the idealism of those past modernities, including even those stigmatised today, such as the Utopias of the twentieth-century Modern Movement, can give us indirect inspiration in our own urgent task for the future: that of reforming the materialistic anarchy of Clone City.

TOWARDS A NEOTECHNIC SOCIETY

As Clone City's central social dynamic is one of fragmentation, breaking down society into divided or competing producers and consumers, any reintegrative reform has to focus on a new concept of the active citizen, supported by new and selective interventions by the state: a tremendous challenge, and opportunity, for our new home-rule government.

The Modernist Age established irrevocably the idea that

everyone has the right to good architecture. But Modernism's credo of material provision left undeveloped the corresponding concept that with that right there also come responsibilities. Today, with the growing concern about blind globalisation, any situation where one group takes all the decisions, whether openly as in Modernism or covertly as in Clone City, and everyone else passively receives or consumes, is unsustainable as a matter of general principle. Today, the building of the city of the future cannot be done by the imposition of overarching principles on the community. It can only be achieved by a change in outlook on the part of the community itself. We cannot do without rules and regulations, but these must come second to the commitment of the people themselves. In this context, the turn-of-century ideas of early Modernists such as Geddes, with their relative freedom from the preoccupations of mass organisation and scientific bureau-cracy, may be of some relevance to us. Geddes's concept of the classless aristo-democratised citizen seemed at the time almost absurdly Utopian, at the dawn of a century of mass confrontation. And, of course, his movement was to be directed by a theocratic elite based in a 'cloister'. But now, with the breakdown of rigid class divisions, perhaps it can help us reconcile the Postmodern marketplace city with the Modernist social city.

We today can effectively build on the aristo-democratic concept, drawing on the more recent experiences both of Glasgow and of Geddes's own culture city of Edinburgh. From Glasgow's pioneer-ing housing associations and community action groups of the 1970s, including especially the Gorbals anti-dampness campaign, have come the passion and popular commitment that would ini-tially make possible a participatory architecture of community. From Edinburgh has come the rejection of class warfare, bureaucratic municipal power and architectural confrontation that would make possible a new, more inclusive process of city renewal. The later career of Robert Matthew reflected this Geddesian ethos of continuity and reconciliation, in its evolution from a Modernist architectural-social determinism to an environ-mentalist, conservationist ethos: the Edinburgh New Town

Shale-mining bing, Broxburn

The King's Knot, Stirling

Conservation Committee, which he founded in 1970, attempted to combine cultural and social commitment in its concentration on the tattered fringe of slum housing on the New Town's edge. In 1969, Richard Holloway, then a young and activist minister in the capital, hailed the growing 'revolt of the amateurs, who love cities, love houses, understand the poetry of their town, and are determined that their environment will not be decided for them by either profiteer or expert.'[24]

For Geddes, the aristo-democratic reconciliation of classes was to be accompanied by a repudiation of Palaeotechnic materialism. For us, a century later, that also involves a recognition of the obsolescence of the twentieth century's claims of a direct correspondence between architecture and social progress – the architectural determinism explicit in much Modernist argumentation, and still implicit in Clone City's community rhetoric. The success of the Modernist drive to build homes means that designers no longer have to make a choice between affirming poverty (by building economical, utilitarian new urban environments) or fleeing from it (through garden-city planning), as they did in the early twentieth century. Certainly, the makers of the built environment can still contribute to the fight against social inequality, but this can only be through negotiating initiatives or practical planning skills that do not necessarily, of themselves, produce environments of spatial and architectural quality. The same even applies to green design principles, such as efficient insulation of housing. These can make a significant contribution to the technical and social excellence of the built environment, but there is no necessary connection between them and spatial or architectural quality. The caravan-park environment of the pioneering Findhorn ecological settlement, or the industrialised chaos of much urban public-transport infrastructure, are hardly different from Clone City.

But the rejection of doctrines of immediate material reformism, and of socialism's demands for more state provision and spending, do not add up to an abandonment of social idealism in the city. In fact, the very reverse is true. The nineteenth-century critic John

Clone City

Ruskin argued that, as from people, 'we require from buildings . . . two kinds of goodness: first, the doing their practical duty well: then that they be graceful and pleasing in doing it; which last is itself another form of duty.'[25] In today's culture, with inequality measured in terms of environment and information as much as material provision, Clone City's debasement and fragmentation itself constitutes a dereliction of collective duty, a profound inequality and injustice. In the zones of social and economic exclusion that have sprung up across the present-day Clone City – largely concentrated in postwar housing schemes – the lack of environmental quality is one of the worst aspects of deprivation. This is not so much because of any inherent aesthetic ugliness, as some of the most stigmatised outer Glasgow housing schemes of the 1950s are physically almost identical to popular areas of the early New Towns, but because of a more insidious relationship of alienation between dwellers on the one hand and the environments on the other. Beautiful cities are a profound good in their own right, but that beauty is not just a matter of empty aestheticism. The question is ultimately one of identity, especially of democratic identity. The process of committing people to the places where they live is ultimately one of allowing people to fulfil their democratic rights. The task of a twenty-first-century Neotechnic vision of the city must be to replace today's materialistic and mechanistic framework, with its artificial schisms between different groups of makers, by a democracy of building, within which diverse interests can work together for justice and integrity in the environment. We must try to reunite image and reality, signifier and signified, through action – through the active redistribution of environmental quality.

The inclusive social scope of the narrative city demands an overall vision of collective and, indeed, redistributive justice in the built environment, so that cheaply built and badly maintained social housing projects such as Easterhouse or Wester Hailes can become as inspiring to inhabit as the old elite areas of Kelvinside or the Edinburgh New Town. Our aim must be to secure equity without the mass homogeneity of the 1950s, and excellence without the spatial inequality of the nineteenth century; to lavish attention and debate not just on new parliament buildings and art galleries but on the ordinary environments of the people. And in serving the social and spiritual needs of the people, we also serve the needs of the nation's long-term democratic cohesion and economic prosperity, in securing a built environment with a genuinely secure and rooted identity. By putting the horse before the cart, both can proceed forwards.

To those still dedicated to the grand promises of material betterment of socialism or technocratic capitalism, this formula of ethically based regeneration might seem wordy and vacuous. But the age of state socialism is now over, and the emptiest rhetoric is that of collectivist mass provision. The state, having given up its old powers in the built environment as elsewhere, is freed to assume new ones, concerned with selective regulation rather than provision or direct spending, and qualitative rather than quantitative issues. That is a testimony to the potential resilience of state power in the environment. But it is also a testimony to the persistence of ideals of social rights and duties in the environment – the concept that the right of development is a conditional one, which entails an obligation to give back architecture and beauty to the community in return.

The city of Neotechnic democracy demands not only social solidarity in the environment of today, but solidarity over time, with our heritage and with the future. Once the linear scramble of materialist Progress is abandoned, then much more flexible connections can be made in all directions. It is here that the real relevance of the green movement emerges, in its insistence on the need for collective moral obligation to be both synchronous (towards others at the present) and diachronous (over time). Everybody involved in making the city is bound together by mutual responsibilities. The fight for justice and responsibility in the built environment is one that links the generations. The monumental cultural-spatial legacy of the Scottish city influences the ways in which we can react to the challenge of globalisation – for example, by deterring rampantly individualistic solutions of a

North American or Belgian kind – but does not dictate our actions. We cannot predict the material needs of those who are to come. All that is certain is that our own immediate needs will be obsolete and irrelevant to them. Our legacy to them will be the substance of the environments we build – so long as we set out to build enduringly and nobly. The Greek historian Thucydides boasted that his book was 'conceived as a possession for all time, rather than as an object for immediate gratification'.[26] We cannot hope to build for all time, but let us at least aspire to build for future generations, as past generations built for us.

EDUCATION AND ENVIRONMENT

In today's Clone City, people have no conception that the environment does not just simply happen, but is created by people, for good or bad. Can the education system play a role in the quest for a society with higher aspirations for the building of the city? At the moment, within the official education system, postmodernity's materialistic split between mechanical banality and empty images is faithfully reflected. Within most school curricula, architecture is treated as a technical matter, like road surveying, with *utilitas* and *firmitas* segregated as purely mechanical specialisms, while any emphasis on *uenustas* is bound up with the heritage industry and its image-led marketing campaigns such as the cult of Mackintosh. Considering the richness of our actual architectural heritage, it is ironic that it should be misused for the purposes of active spiritual impoverishment.

But the history of late nineteenth- and early twentieth-century Scottish architecture also contains an alternative strand of educational thinking, an integrated perspective which has transcended the polemical twists and turns of those years, including the Modern Movement. At the end of the last century, Geddes almost single-handedly set about the revival of mural painting in Scotland, in the hope that decorating homes, schools and workplaces with scenes of national history and legend might help regenerate modern materialistic society. He railed at an educational system which tried to develop 'minds . . . in the stupefying blankness of white-washed schoolrooms', and called instead for the raising of a 'paradise . . . blazoned in gold and colour'.[27] At first, that vision could be put into practice only in isolated cases. For example, it was realised in Phoebe Traquair's glorious murals for St Mary's Cathedral Song School in Edinburgh (1888–92), which today still form the backdrop for the singing lessons of pupils at Scotland's only national music school. Robert Matthew was an outspoken advocate of extending this quality of experience to the population at large. In 1953, for instance, he argued that his own love of architecture had been inspired by the beauty of a Robert Adam mansion in which he spent his early schooldays; and he asserted that education must decisively engage with the aesthetics of the city, to foster the sense of architecture as a 'living experience': the responsibility for city-building 'cannot be pinned on the few; it must derive from the many'.[28] And in 1970, he expanded that call to link with the beginnings of the green movement, advocating a crash programme of school and university teaching of environ-mental issues.[28]

Matthew's arguments show us that, in the drive towards a civilisation founded on an integrity of shared ideals rather than on the diktats of rules and abstract moral principles, there is a vital connection between buildings, as an enduring material nar-rative of collective endeavour, and the education of future citizens. If people are to develop the identity with which to combat environ-mental injustice, knowledge is the first prerequisite. But even in his age, the Modernist Age, society was still too authoritarian in its organisation of the city to be able to excite the commitment of all its members. It was only in the wake of the participatory movements of the 1970s and later that a new range of educational initiatives, both public and private, began to emerge, aimed at fostering a climate of intergenerational commitment to the built environment. In its last years of existence, Strathclyde Regional Council started to introduce integrated design courses as part of its primary and secondary school curricula. After the abolition of the council in 1996, this initiative was expanded under the same

personnel in Glasgow's new Lighthouse centre for architecture
and design, where a quarter of the entire floorspace is devoted to
children – a built-in 'children's city' intended to involve school
pupils, and, through them, their adult relatives. The aspiration
of Stuart MacDonald, director of the Lighthouse, is that 'we get
the kids in during the week, and they'll then bring their parents
back at the weekend!'[29]

In the task of creating a democracy of building which spans
the whole of society as well as spanning the generations, today's
conservation movement is of special relevance. It is relevant not
only for the obvious reason that it makes an ethical link between
past and future, but also for its more subtle social significance.
This is a movement whose social base has gone far beyond the
gestural crudeness which still bedevils some new community architecture. This is a genuinely popular movement concerned with
quality rather than quantity in the built environment, and embracing intellectualised debate and regulation as well as passionate
campaigning and – most important of all – an entrenched appa-
ratus of educational proselytising that is throughly diffused across
society. At the moment, conservation is the only environmental
agency pursuing a large-scale social movement of education for
communal identity. Compared with this complex and organic
formula, the most common formula of new, community-based
regeneration today – the blowing up of tower blocks and the
building of brick shanty towns in their place – seems about as
modern and sophisticated a problem-solving approach as the
burning of witches in the seventeenth century!

Within conservation theory, to ensure that the past is properly
handed on to the future, the community takes special powers of
control over private property and development rights. But there
is nothing in the logic of the argument to prevent it being applied,
with equal force, to the pursuit of excellence in new architecture
and building, to secure cities worthy of being handed on to future
generations. We have been able to create pride across the whole
of society in what exists, in the 'old', to the extent of indignantly
defending it against blind market forces – despite the bewildering

Muirhouse, Edinburgh

Corstorphine, Edinburgh

variety of conflicting views as to what heritage is for. There is no logical reason why this organic consensus should not be achieved in aspirations for the future of our environment.

Ironically, as we have seen, some conservationists often fail to grasp the full implications of this concept of intergenerational equity. Constrained by a simplistic concept of linear progress and modernity, the Morrisian tradition erects a rigid demarcation around the past and diverts its energies into tirades against 'sham restorations' – despite the fact that a creatively restored old building may be just as valuable to future generations as a repaired one! German and Austrian conservation theorists, such as Alois Riegl, avoided these self-inflicted divisions by recognising a much wider range of criteria of heritage than mere oldness of fabric, including an artistic value, a historical documentary value, and a social and material use value or *Gebrauchswert*. From a religious perspective, too, it is clear that the only viable concept of heritage is the monumental rather than the antiquarian. Speaking of a restoration scheme for one of Scotland's cathedrals, its provost argued that 'heritage is about a living, dynamic concept, not a preservation society for mausoleums'; the duty of the church is 'to rejoice in and treasure the heritage that is ours, but not to fossilise it . . . or to render it so wind- and water-tight that the world cannot get in.'[30]

If we, like those commentators, recognise that old buildings are just one element in a wider framework of relationships over place and over time in the built environment, we can begin to quietly reorganise the great narrative of city-making. We can begin to disentangle today's disparate agencies of production and consumption from their present commodified setting. We can start to re-politicise the process of consumption, binding freedom and choice to responsibility, and press on towards a radical restructuring and ennoblement of production, yoking the building industry and the professions into a coordinated instrument of environmental excellence, in the sense both of material social solidarity and of the beauty of the everyday environment. It must be the job of the state, no longer itself directly involved in mass building, to hold this new balance between demand and supply, consumption and production, in the building of the city.

To Postmodern critics who might dismiss this call as hollow rhetoric or as a cloak for the self-aggrandisement of intellectuals, we need only point to the well established and wide community support for conservation. No one today could credibly argue that the consensus against demolition of listed monuments is a fraudulent disguise for elite interests, and that it should therefore be abandoned. Conservation has made a big and growing mark on our cities and their economies – not always for the good – and it could not conceivably be described as a shallow fantasy of the ruling classes. Dare we hope that the same consensus could be built up, in the coming decades, in support of the future of our cities? Emancipated consumers and producers working together towards a common vision of the city, under the sponsorship of our new home-rule government: that could be the first step towards a real renewal of freedom and order, a true democracy of building.

ARISTO-DEMOCRATIC CITIZENS: THE ENNOBLEMENT OF CONSUMPTION AND PRODUCTION

In contrast to past centuries, when collective visions of the city were a matter for a relatively small elite, today they can be achieved only with the support and commitment of everyone. But the concept of consumption by all has been immeasurably complicated by the late twentieth century's dissolution of the old concepts of authoritative society, lumpen classes and mass culture – the cement which re-embedded industrial civilisation. This dissolution has been quietest, yet most important, in the formerly private area of the family, where the old, introverted norms and relationships have been torn apart. The most obvious and easily quantifiable consequences of this have been in the areas of demography and housing demand, where a wave of new, single-person households has been created, and a quarter of a million dwellings have been added to Scotland's predicted housing need between 1996 and 2006. But a more subtle change has been under way in the social and ethical concepts of community and identity. Many have condemned the undermining of family structures as a destructive factor. But equally, it holds out the promise of a great liberation. For it has begun to burst open the rigid cage of natalism – the old moral-racial doctrine of prosperity and wholeness through national population growth – with its stifling normative rhetoric of family fertility and decency.

Community in the built environment is no longer necessarily something that can be created only by lining up the little orderly units of 'families' and providing them with material goods. Now the making of the city can begin to be accepted as a continuous process or experience, in which no one's role is privileged as a unique 'maker'. The potential for this has partly been laid at a basic organisational level: for example, the shifting of subsidies from dwellings to their occupiers has personalised the whole financial basis of social housing. And it is has also been laid within broader cultural attitudes to the city. No longer do buildings simply constrain the subject by surfaces, boundaries, gazes, but equally the reverse applies: the users appropriate their environment.

Under Postmodernity, the concept of the culture city has been visualised in narrowly economistic terms of image marketing and consumption. But, as Geddes suggested, the same term can equally be used as a definition of civic community. Now, it may be possible to begin moving beyond the model of basic neighbourhood improvement to wider regeneration, creating deeper alliances between the 'enabled' and the professions which transcend the old class castes of 'us and them'. Here, once again, Glasgow is beginning to take the lead, with the emergence of a new generation of strategically orientated community associations. In place of the short-termism of the 1970s and 1980s, and the feelings of insecurity among lay committee members in dealing with architects, now there is increasingly a position of user control. There is no denial of the existence of power, but a change in the way it is used. To Glasgow community housing leaders such as Fraser Stewart or

Clone City

Rob Joiner, the divisive materialism of old-style working-class socialist ideology is obsolete and irrelevant. The task is, rather, to extend the passion and commitment of the private, personal and local to a public scale, to the point where it can ultimately inspire the regeneration of the whole city. No longer is it enough just to receive or preserve. People whose predecessors were passive consumers of ready-made identities have now become active producers or contributors of identity. The criteria for the new generation of community projects are those of inspiration, integrity and beauty: the questions of leadership, of being a patron of architecture in the widest sense. The earlier tentative solutions, leaning heavily on the crutch of the 'traditional tenement', are yielding to more modern, radical visions.

This new, democratic consumption process is not something to be done on the cheap or swept under the carpet. It is a process as pregnant with collective aspiration as any of the old, elite types of patronage, such as the building of merchants' suburbs or commercial *palazzi*. Community groups have to constantly lift their sights and conduct themselves with growing intellectual integrity, opening themselves to public debate and scrutiny: we cannot build enduringly beautiful cities by local plebiscite. 'Community' no longer means hole-in-corner or patronisingly exempt from criticism. For a local community group to deface a regenerated housing area with brick boxes is now every bit as unacceptable as for a property developer to demolish a neo-classical villa in an elite suburb. The debate about the city must embrace both power and art, or we lose both. In the city of social narrative, there need be no conflict between the idealistic quest to order the world for the future through the construction of noble places, and the real life of the streets today. As artist Alan Johnston argues, the mountain of aspiration rises directly from the collective plain of everyday human affairs.

While Clone City's regime of concealed materialistic power is already being challenged from the outside by the creation of community alliances of users and inhabitants, another, possibly even more significant change is under way within the production machine itself, in response to a number of unexpected and potentially liberating effects of globalisation. Here, yet again, we can build on what is already happening, in Eutopian fashion, rather than having to tear down and start from new.

During the Historicist Age, the laissez-faire system of city-building balanced the interests of producers, consumers and the (narrowly defined, elite) community. Although the mass production of everyday housing environments became dominated by a new kind of large builder-developer, like James Steel in Edinburgh or John Mactaggart in Glasgow, these private builders worked willingly within a system of collective architectural regulation intended to safeguard the long-term environmental quality of the Scottish city. The twentieth-century era of mass discipline tipped the scales towards production. Within the building industry, the old, more economical system of separate trades was replaced by those of the powerful main contractor or of state-controlled direct labour. Social building activity, often in the form of design-and-build contracts, was heavily subsidised by the state. At first, the strong collective ideals of public building maintained a collective restraint, however mundane some of the resulting mass environments may have been. But with the decline in social corporatism and state subsidies from the 1980s, the way seemed open to an almost unrestrained producer power, especially in the massed building of clone homes by private builders. All that had apparently happened was the exchange of one type of monopoly for another, with the proportions of public and private housing output in the 1950s (90 per cent and 10 per cent) exactly reversed by the 1990s.

Robert Matthew, presenting the Saltire Awards for housing design in 1969, predicted that speculative builder-led development of new communities in Scotland 'would be a disaster, unless there is a fundamental change in the attitude of private enterprise towards standards of design'. And the story of deregulated mass housing during the late 1980s and 1990s seemed, at first glance, to confirm those fears. Some Scottish speculative housebuilders, such as Cruden or Mactaggart & Mickel, made valiant attempts to revive the old social ethos of nineteenth-century building entrepreneurship in the planning of their developments. But other, more voracious builders, diversifying into the 'Scottish regional market' from southern England, chose to revive a different type of nineteenth-century capitalist attitude: the opportunism of noxious industry, the smash-and-grab attitude of opencast mining or chemical dumping, of taking the profit and leaving the eventual work of decontamination to someone else. These confrontational attitudes were not actually the fault of the firms themselves. They were only doing their job, flowing into an intellectual and ethical vacuum, and not, it should be said, making large profits by doing so: the most unattractive developments were in many respects the cheapest and most basic ones.

But the process of modernity cannot be declared, by decree, complete at any single point. The monolithic power of the state as patron of building has already broken up; and now it is the turn of the powerful builders, whether working as contractors or speculatively, to feel the effects of change. With the inexorable underlying shift in potential power from producer to consumer, take-it-or-leave-it trade-offs between building performance and longer-term interests, including environmental quality, are increasingly questioned.[31] The authority of the centrally controlled design-and-build contract has sharply declined. And main contracting has become far less monolithic, with the customisation and internationalisation of the procurement and building process in the most prestigious public or commercial projects, as the vast lists of subcontractors outside any major building site show. Even in housing, although still largely a craft-based industry, there are gradual changes, with the growing demand from home-buyers for flexibility and personal input into house layout and design, and the pressure to cut costs in design and construction. Some responsible and ethically aware developers, especially smaller firms in 'niche' urban regeneration schemes, but also some larger ones, are moving towards a more responsive approach, in which production choice becomes an enriching rather than impoverishing factor, and the sharp barriers between design, production and consumption

Gartcosh Steel Mill, Lanarkshire

Haddington

are broken down – the same trends already established in community-based housing, but here linked to the supply as well as the demand side, and tapping into the far greater potential of private-based investment.

Already, some social housing developments by private firms involve a vast endeavour in professional and contractual effort, financing and procurement, production of detailed plans, and general tenurial and architectural diversity. The contrast could not be starker with both the highly standardised production-led procedures of both Clone City's brick boxes and the huge 1950s state housing schemes of tenements. An even more innovative example of this kind of social entrepreneurship is the experimental group of modernist blocks sponsored in the Glasgow 1999 'Homes for the Future' demonstration project by speculative builders, including John Dickie Construction and Mactaggart & Mickel, with support from government agency Scottish Homes. Previously, the kind of lavish attention to detail seen in these experimental housing projects was possible only in buildings for the rich, especially during the nineteenth-century era of greatest Scottish wealth (relatively speaking). At that time, great things were achieved by a combination of enlightened, demanding clients and a production process of checks and balances. Now, with these beginnings of a democratically integrated system of developers and consumers, the possibility opens up of generalising this ethos of care throughout the community.

For architecture and architects, the new and more complex relationship between producers and consumers brings with it the possibility of a vital intermediary role, as a source of inspiration and clarification. Architectural practice, like the rest of society, is wide open to the forces of decomposition emanating from the private realm, from the home. The gradual erosion of male dominance within the profession undermines the old unitary vocational notion of the architectural career. The opportunity opens up of collaborative relationships in all directions. On the one hand, there are new ideals of interaction with artists, new processes of intellectual fusion rather different from the organic crafts vision of collaboration in the physical putting together of a building, or the Modernist multidisciplinary concepts of 'comprehensive environmental intelligence'. On the other hand, the demarcations of production are beginning to break down in innovative projects which carry the values of design into the production and building system, corroding the cheap-and-fast approach from within. Although today, in contrast to the old separate-trades system of direct control, the designer may have to retreat several stages back from project management, and may thus lose some control at the most perfectionist level of detail, this loss is counterbalanced by the possibilities of winning the respect of the other players in the new, more complex social system of city-making, by fusing architecture with a wider intellectualisation of the processes of development.

STATE OF ORDER

If we want to ensure that any renewal of the relationship between design and production will add up to more than empty words, it would be naive in the extreme to rely solely on the innate idealism and righteousness of human nature, without the support of checks and balances. Here too, fortunately, there is no need to invent any new mechanism of external arbitration or regulation, as one is already to hand: the state.

Whatever the particular economic or social institutions of any civilisation at any particular time, all have shared a general faith in the potential ability of the physical environment to express the aspirations of the ruling power. In contemporary Scotland, the international spread of capitalist globalisation and user appropriation has not abolished the role of the state, but has refocused its potential scope. With the obsolescence of the old, war-like campaigns of mass intervention and direct provision, there is now the opportunity for new kinds of flexible regulation, reducing the state's controls in some area while expanding its involvement in others. So far, in Scotland, the shift towards a more hands-off role has been an across-the-board policy. The decline in state spending and provision has been matched by a decline in state regulation and control. In this, our country contrasts with a number of others. For example, the Netherlands has succeeded in combining effective market liberalisation with a continuing role for the state as a regulator and guarantor of the quality of life. There, the municipal *Welstandscommissies* (quality committees) assess building projects through a truly Vitruvian balance of the practical and the aesthetic.

The Dutch experience shows that the move from public to private housing provision need not mean urban chaos, if there is a collective commitment to the city. And in fact, most of the successful aspects of capitalist society since Adam Smith have been achieved by a measure of regulation, to harness their fundamental urge towards freedom and individualism. Within nineteenth-century Scotland, the extreme order of the period's urban developments, whether in everyday Glasgow tenements or Edinburgh's Moray Estate, was the product of a system of entrepreneurial builders working within tight private architectural direction. But it was also guaranteed by external regulation, either by the private stipulations of the feudal superior or by the municipal regulation of building by Dean of Guild Courts.

Those kinds of careful controls were only sustainable within the relatively limited scale of the environments of the pre-1914 ruling classes. Today, with the need to extend urban cohesion across the whole community, a broader-brush regulation framework seems inevitable. Does the interventionist Modernist Age provide us with a more useful working model? Some aspects of that interventionism are clearly not relevant to us, and indeed are more closely affiliated to the values of Clone City: for instance, the concern for short-term mass provision, the 'numbers game'. But alongside these, there were other Modernist state initiatives of large scale, such as the New Towns and regional planning programmes, which were equally concerned with long-term strategies of renewal, and with the fostering of places of enduring spiritual resonance.

The state has lost the ability and desire to directly plan and produce the built environment on that kind of grand scale. But what it has been left with instead is a very large carrot and stick with which to stimulate others. It can both subsidise and regulate on a far wider scale than could public authorities in any period prior to 1914. But in recent years, the two arms of policy have become disconnected from one another.

The regulation role has gradually, but inexorably atrophied. Following the end of the Modernist era of grand regional plans for active reconstruction, the development plan system has still allowed local authority planners a potentially detailed control over land use, a control which extends, through local plans and design briefs, to cover the appearance of developments, and changes to existing buildings.[32] These controls, like the increasingly exacting regulation of building standards, are now seen as essentially reactive and demand-led, and are at their most successful in dealing with micro-issues, such as the maintaining of grey facing materials in 'Granite Aberdeen'. But their effectiveness in wider tasks, such as the long-standing ban on building in the green belts around cities, has been thrown into question by the 1996 local government reorganisation, which abolished most of the strategic regional authorities within the Central Belt and replaced them by a mosaic of competing smaller authorities. As we saw above, Strathclyde Region was the source of some of today's most significant initiatives in urban environmental education. In the field of strategic planning, its abolition has left a gaping hole which is currently papered over by an unwieldy joint board, the Glasgow and Clyde Valley Structure Plan Joint Committee. At a national level, the scrutiny of all major building projects by the Royal Fine Art Commission provides a valuable overview, but in a purely hortatory form. Only in the heritage field, in the case of listed buildings and conservation areas, do central and local government collaborate in a comprehensive system of proactive regulation with teeth, a potential precedent to which we shall return shortly.

Corresponding to this atrophying of the function of control, there has been a burgeoning of subsidy activity by both central and local agencies, as part of a more and more overtly market-dominated system of economic promotion. In housing and urban regeneration, private builders have up to now been massively supported by central government through public grants, housing benefits and owner-occupation tax breaks. The cost of owner-occupation in Scotland, as a percentage of annual income, is (for instance) only one-fifth of that in Switzerland. Up to now, much of the effect of this capitalist indirect provision, no less than socialist direct provision before it, has been one of urban fragmentation rather than enhancement. For example, Scottish Homes's Grants for Rent and Ownership ('GRO-Grants'), introduced in 1990 to 'bring more choice' to low-cost housing, played until recently a key supporting role in the spread of Clone City.[33] With the enthusiastic support of the last Tory government, they fuelled the mass demolition of Modern Movement environments and the unrestrained outpouring of brick clone homes in their place. And the nexus of publicly subsidised roads and new exurban housing and commerce only compounded the damage.

Local authorities, too, are now jumping on this bandwagon of market-dictated growth. In the new unitary councils, planning departments are increasingly being merged with quasi-entrepreneurial or development functions. Following the dismantling of the two-tier government structure and the restructuring of urban regeneration aid into a competitive bidding process, competition between the new authorities, along with their allied local enterprise companies, has become steadily fiercer. The smallest councils are increasingly susceptible to developer pressure for ugly low-density sprawl, not only on Clydeside but also in other small Central Belt authorities. In the opinion of the Royal Fine Art Commission, many smaller authorities now 'see themselves as developers first and foremost'.[34]

But now, just as in the case of the building industry, things are changing: the state itself is being transformed. Up until now, the structure of government in Scotland has been dominated by a combination of administrative civil service devolution and strong local government autonomy – a system which well suited the mid-twentieth century's combination of mass democracy and mass bureaucracy. Now, a structure of political home-rule democracy in the central state, with integrated government and legislature, is being put in its place – at the very same time that the local authorities are being stripped of their strategic planning role and converted into local capitalist investment agencies. At the moment, the prolonged debates about the parliament building have channelled the assumed architectural impact of home rule into the field of culture buildings and institutions, in the same way that devolution in Catalonia brought an explosion in the building of culture city institutions.

Hopefully, Scottish debates about the architectural role of the central state can be lifted beyond this essentially Postmodern trade in images of representation, and can address the crisis of Clone City as a whole. But what is emphatically not needed in this country is a politically motivated manipulation of particular projects for pork-barrel purposes, or higher public spending, in isolation, as a precondition for the recovery of environmental justice in the Scottish city. Rather, what is already being spent by the state on the built environment could be used much more effectively, and, even, more economically, by adopting a more careful approach. For example, covering the urban periphery with little, separate brick boxes and their attendant service and transport networks, as we do in Scotland, is very unlikely to be the most cost-effective way of providing social housing! In Ireland, by contrast, the flexibility of decision-making in a small country makes it possible to devise ingenious tax breaks to pump-prime individual regeneration projects, fuelling investment and, ultimately, prosperity. Might it be that, by sparking off creative and self-reliant responses, by inspiring the growth of innovative initiatives by government or philanthropic initiatives by Scottish industrialists, the possible move away from Westminster funding under home rule may actually work to Scotland's long-term cultural and economic benefit?

THE REBIRTH OF PLANNING

The key to the effective use of state powers in the built environment lies in a reinvigoration of the ideal of planning. Whereas today's two alternative approaches – the development control measures of the technicians, and the economic promotion systems of the marketing experts – look only to the short term, this must be a strategic vision, like those of the Historicist and Modernist Ages. But it cannot simply resurrect either of the two previous phases of controls, whether the Historicist Age's high-quality but elitist systems or the Modernist Age's vast, Utopian schemes. Both are now equally obsolete and inaccessible.

Within Modernist planning, it was assumed that the identity of town and region could be reshaped into completely new community configurations. Clone City's neo-capitalistic reaction against that kind of statist planning has retained its rampant materialism while discarding the overall vision. The new town programme's centrifugal population movement continues in a directionless and socially divisive form, as an atomised, market-led sprawl. Faced with today's new Darwinian chaos of public agencies and local authorities wrestling with each other in the mud, a new and enlightened state regulation framework seems inevitable.

As in the Netherlands today, so, in this respect, in Scotland tomorrow: economic liberalism, to succeed, must go hand-in-hand with environmental justice and order. Our greater freedoms must be protected from the blind tyranny of the market. There has to be some kind of return to structure, to hierarchy, to identity, to the concerted pursuit of environmental order for all. But this must be an order, it is now clear, of a different and more complex kind that that of the Modernist Age: an order made up of the free association of the local and the cosmopolitan, and of the participatory and regulatory; an order shaped by the poetic as much as by the rational or material, and inspired by the old as much as by the new; an order owing much to the principles of comprehensive and proactive regulation already established in conservation, with its concern for material assets and creative architectural rootedness; an environmental order of a synoptic yet also specific kind, as presaged in Geddes's concept of the city as an organism, and in the place-rooted elements of Modernist planning, such as Frank Mears's South-Eastern Plan of the 1940s, with its call for planned community-building based on the nuclei of historic burghs and planned villages; an order based on a new, flexible hierarchy, with land use and transport infrastructure at the most basic level, and detailed design built up on top of that.

The application of any new urban order of this kind must be both general and specific, combining overarching frameworks or plans for the general run of uncontentious cases with the ability to examine difficult or problematic ones in detail. Following principles first enunciated by Geddes, the conventions of official planning this century have advocated a staged process, beginning with survey and passing on then to a development plan, based on land use zoning and infrastructure provision. During the period of two-tier local government (1975–96), development plans were divided into structure plans – the responsibility of the regions – and more specific local plans. It is at the level of structure plans that the most fundamental locational conflicts of city and region may be addressed – especially the tension between the laissez-faire dynamism of the periphery city and the containment and context of the old city, and the role of transportation infrastructure in regulating that relationship – for example, in any move to curb car-mobile sprawl.

On paper, there is very little wrong with this system. What has been lacking in recent years is the will to make comprehensive or active use of it, to coordinate the different agencies to arrive at joined-up solutions. We should therefore proceed cautiously with reform. The first step, possibly by an initiative of national structure planning by the new Scottish government, must be to correct the worst abuses of the present system, in its encouragement of rampant parcellisation, car dependency and social polarisation. Public authorities should be restored into a collaborative rather than competitive relationship, building on each other's strengths. More than that: it may be necessary for the Scottish government

Glenboig

Netherlee

to take a fresh and urgent look at Central Belt local-authority boundaries, many of which, after all, were only drawn for obsolete party political reasons by a previous government. Solutions to the worst disparities in environmental problems, especially around Glasgow, are now actively obstructed by local boundaries, and a radical policy of redistribution may be the only way to break out. Geddes argued that cities should be seen above all as Centres of Life rather than centres of bureaucratic administration. Now, with home rule upon us, the time when cities must be equated with rigid institutions and boundaries – whether municipal-socialist or competitive-capitalist – may at last be over. Only by throwing down the defence fortifications of antagonistic municipal power can the creative forces of civic life and urban democracy be set free.

Supported by these general organisational reforms, as well as by the long-promised shift of government emphasis from private to public transport (an issue we will return to in Chapter 5), we can begin to put together more specific measures to address the random parcellisation of urban environments, the restriction of the civic interest to a limited public realm, and the car-fuelled encouragement of spatial polarisation between income groups. Our aim must be to reclaim the whole of our cities as common space for all. But nothing at all can be done without active public-authority zoning of land use, to restrain laissez-faire nomadism of land values and uses, on the principle established first in 1940s green-belt designations. Land-use zoning is only a preliminary step, a technical instrument, towards the wider goal of order in what we build. Here, too, the state must be prepared to intervene, to help build the numerous local initiatives into a wider national process of regeneration for the entire community. This is not a matter of the specifying of particular styles, like the Prussian street blocks encouraged in post-reunification Berlin. Such attempts today, like Modern Movement command planning before them, invariably become bogged down in polemical controversy: it is not the task of planners to dictate design. What is at issue is not authoritarian order, but the ordering of freedom: the securing of an overall integrity of form, and its general relation to the society and economy of city and nation.

In the Modernist years, the value of authenticity was acknowledged by a struggle for homogeneity and essentialism in design. In 1967, for example, the American Institute of Architects applauded the 'consistency' of Cumbernauld New Town's 'grey monochrome with occasional colour relief'. They argued that 'monotony' had been avoided by variety in building types, siting and street landscaping.[35] This, in other words, was an imposed order, with elements of variety and freedom designed into it. In the reaction against the Modern Movement, Postmodern Scotland swung away from this designed variety towards a more overt individualism. With the bathwater of Modernist dirigisme, we threw out the baby of authenticity. But as overseas examples like the current dockland regenerations in Amsterdam indicate, it is possible, through a flexible framework of positive aesthetic ordering – not just negative, technical development control – to reconcile the present-day demands for complexity with the openness of classical and Modernist space, and to reconcile our age's demand for freedom within an overall harmony.

What does not follow from the rejection of doctrinaire Modernism, in the context of the Scottish cities and landscape, is the Darwinian argument of the inevitability of instant-gratification rootlessness – the claim of some contemporary architectural commentators that megaplex sprawl is the urbanism of the future, cannot be resisted and so should be welcomed. It is not a matter of preordained inevitability that great cities and towns should have been reduced to competitors wrestling in the mud; and it will be the task of the new Scottish government to see that this state of affairs does not continue.

As with the other Eutopian policies advocated in these pages, we must begin our search for the ideal formula of state intervention not from new, but from what already exists. For our task of reconciling individual freedom with authenticity and consistency, there already exists an important exemplar: the comprehensive system of regulation put into place since the late 1960s in the field of heritage. This framework, operating with a great deal of public support, comprises three elements: a national-government policy-making and oversight element, run by Historic Scotland; a local implementation system, run by local planning authorities and specialist conservation architects; and a voluntary sector, which provides informed public comment and education at both the national and local levels. During the period of the introduction of the system, especially in the 1970s, central government had to play a more direct role, but since then, implementation has been steadily devolved to local level. The regulation of the new built environment should be remodelled on the analogy of this effective system of heritage regulation. Here we emphasise that the relevance of heritage control for new architecture, within our argument, is strictly as an analogy, not as a direct example. We have no wish to expand conservation controls in their own right!

What could be the equivalent to this system in the field of new building? The local and voluntary conservation sector already has a ready-made equivalent: the enlightened community input discussed above. The official regulation system of the future would most logically have two tiers. In effect, the ground has already been prepared for this by the abolition of the regional councils which (in the Central Belt) formed a middle tier of planning oversight. Up to now, the strategic role played by the regional councils has been left vacant – a gap which the new Scottish government must step in to fill. The first tier would be a local implementation level, run by local authorities through the medium of regulated master-planning of individual projects and areas in accordance with development plans, and coordinated with a national and local system of limited outline-design competitions for all major public or publicly subsidised projects: in the Netherlands, local authorities are able to regulate free-market housing development by price controls and by putting developers in touch with architects. The second tier would be a national policy level of regulation, under the oversight of a standing state commission of the Scottish government: an expanded and reinforced version of the existing Royal Fine Art Commission and the former regional planning authorities, with direct input into legislation on the built environment and into local-authority structure planning, and the power, at first, to intervene directly and impose solutions in important individual cases, as a means of establishing consistency and precedent.

Eventually, on the model of the Historic Scotland/local-authority relations within heritage, that close national oversight could be relaxed, once the system of local regulation and national/local design competition had built up to a critical level of efficiency, leaving the long-term role of the central government element as one of policy formulation and coordination of problematic issues or building types, or regional planning issues. This is an approach already potentially visible, for example, in the government's appointment in 1996 of an architect-adviser to assess new road proposals, following the refusal of a series of utilitarian, engineer-designed schemes by the Royal Fine Art Commission. The potentially regulatory implications of other government-subsidised programmes, such as those of Scottish Homes or the enterprise companies, should also be brought under the direct oversight of the new regulatory regime.

Even if we regard the sweeping coordinating machinery of the Netherlands as beyond our reach and inappropriate to a country that has not been wrested from the sea, other Northern European countries have also come to see selective state intervention as a powerful weapon in the fight for environmental justice. In Ireland, the Minister of Housing and Urban Renewal has intervened to calm and channel haphazard urbanisation, by formulating binding architectural guidelines for all publicly subsidised buildings and important private developments. Even more important, the government-sponsored Heritage Council has brought together a wide range of initiatives on the built and natural environment under the overall banner of intergenerational responsibility. In Norway, the agency *Norsk Form* and the Ministry of Culture take proactive and proselytising measures in cooperation with local authorities, including the encouragement of better design in diverse building types of major townscape and landscape impact, such as petrol stations and scattered housing developments: in 1996, the Minister of Cultural Affairs declared that 'the environment is a public space. The right developers have been given to use public space, entails a corresponding moral obligation to give something to the community in return. That something is architecture.'[36]

Perhaps the most ambitious attempt to relate environmental identity to democracy is a commission recently set up by the Swedish government to investigate ways in which architecture can itself be used as a resource in the democratic process. This exciting initiative, run by the National Architecture Museum with the Ministry of Culture and Education, treats the whole of the built environment to date, including the vast twentieth-century planned social achievements of the Swedish welfare state, as a resource to help in the fostering of a democratic future. Here in Scotland, the coming world of home-rule government will offer us all an opportunity for active re-engagement with one of the most real issues of our daily lives – the question of what kind of cities we want to inhabit. If we use this opportunity well, we will not only have put in place at home the foundations of a new democracy of building, liberated from market authoritarianism, but will also have contributed to a wider international response to the alienating effects of globalisation.

The Forth Valley at Stirling
Clydeforth: map from the Mears Report
The Clyde Valley at Greenock

4
CLYDEFORTH
Conurbation in Landscape

A great and living city, which would be second to none.[37]

Clone City's fragmentation of urban society is parallelled by its fragmentation of the spatial structure of the city. Thus, any renewal of people must go hand in hand with a renewal of place. It is all very well to call for a rebirth of planning, but that call can only be an abstraction without an active vision to accompany it.

Today's patterns of fragmentation and exclusion echo the dislocations of the past, in the way in which they polarise and dissolve at the same time – spatially, just as much as socially. They set the dense inner areas against the periphery. The former is treated with love and care as the essential city, with its own meticulous spatial formula of continuous, pedestrian-friendly fabric, while the latter is relegated to the status of an amorphous left-over with no controlling vision, a zone passively traversed by car. In the specific context of the Central Belt, this outer growth is left to amorphously overlap the rural frame, while the supposedly essential inner city is further polarised around the two extremes of Glasgow and Edinburgh, the old east-west contrast being corrupted under the influence of local-government reorganisation into a 'bare-knuckle fight' for investment and the building of cultural institutions. Within this market-driven framework, order is now represented by a fundamentalism of the old centre, and the outer edge becomes a place not so much of freedom as of regimented anarchy.

What is lost is any idea of the whole, in either an ideal sense or in the specific context of Central Scotland. But that whole cannot be wished away. Internationally, the city region, with its problems of internal organisation and external definition, represents the

113

key field of contention in the built environment at the end of this century. It is as emblematic of our time as the industrial city was of the nineteenth century. And like the industrial city, its problems are increasingly discussed as a crisis of the uncontrolled reproduction of a generic type, under whatever name – *Zwischenstadt*, Edge City, 'XL', and so forth. Thus the crisis of the Central Belt as a whole, and not just that of its components, is a crisis of cloning; and its solution is a challenge of general as well as specific relevance.

Throughout the discussion which follows, there is a dual, parallel focus: on the one hand, an ideal framework of the whole and its parts; on the other, the constraints of our specific situation in the Central Belt. We have to seek to regenerate the city region in both the abstract and the particular, building on what already exists, in Eutopian fashion, creatively transforming and rescuing our Clone City, rather than repudiating it for another extreme Utopian solution. If we succeed, that success can then contribute in a small way to a more general change from rootless globalism to specific place, from the city of driving Progress to the city of cumulative narrative.

At the level of the ideal city, our first recognition must be that the challenges posed by modernity have not gone away, but remain much the same as ever: to produce environments in which the pressures of modernising change and freedom are given order by integrated spatial ideals. But today an even more flexible approach than before is needed. We have to avoid both fundamentalism and destructive Utopianism. In the light of today's scepticism about the credibility of authoritative or dogmatic formulae, whether of the future or the past, it is simply inadequate to put forward simplistic, unitary litmus tests of quality, or recipes for the recovery of coherence, such as 'the compact city', 'mixed use' or 'the public realm'. These are just as hollow, in the end, as Functionalism's more extravagant slogans of scientific futurism – and a lot less credible than some of the humane aspects of Modernism which actually were realised, such as the strategy of the New Towns, or the building of Modernist interventions in historic burghs. Here, once more, a Eutopian solution demands that we look closely again at what has been achieved during the course of the twentieth century.

Alongside those considerations of the ideal city, we need to work with the specific material we have to hand. For in many cases, the Scottish city or town is literally a City on a Hill. Designers of our urban environments, whether of classical stateliness, picturesque antiquity or flowing Modernist monumentality, have always been able to work with the grain of a highly differentiated landscape, whose restrained sublimity is always perceptible, yet never overwhelming enough to reduce all architecture to dwarfish insignificance. But, just as elsewhere in Europe, the topography of the Scottish urban built environment, after its successive centuries of building 'with' the landscape, can no longer be described simply as a matter of nature. It, too, has become opened out and freed from its constraints to become another artefact of culture. It has become super-enhanced as a theatre of the sublime, through a fertile interaction of the topographic context with the architectural traditions of stone monumentality, and with the radical and renewing concepts of spatial integrity.

As a result, there is, today, no simple definition of the essence of place in the Scottish city, which can provide a clear first statement of order against chaos, or an easy way of re-embedding our cities in their landscape roots. Even in the most fixed and enduring geographical elements – climate, geology, topography – we immediately encounter variable cultural factors which complicate their influence immensely. The reaction to Scotland's relatively equable and changeable climate has taken widely differing forms at different historical stages, varying from the thick-walled castles of the sixteenth century to the complex composite construction of the nineteenth-century tenements. The geological context has been vital in allowing the development of a building tradition whose emphasis on monumental dignity has complemented the variegated natural setting of the Scottish city. But from the mid-nineteenth century, the possibility of obtaining non-local stone by rail, and the demand for precision finish on facades, converted

Inner Ring Road, Glasgow

Stirling Castle and the Wallace Monument

urban building materials from a matter of necessity to one of cus-
tomised image. It is within that cultural and economic framework
of open modernity, separated several times over from any direct
response to the geological setting, that today's debates take place
about the 'Scottish wall' and the 'stone-building tradition'.

These complicating cultural influences allowed the creation of a
succession of cultural-topographic visions which balanced the ideal
and the specific: over centuries, social and spiritual aspiration,
and topographical reality, became inextricably entwined. The
Central Scottish conurbation of today is not the result of a single
essence, but the outcome of the overlaying of many visions. These
first assumed their bipolar east-west form in the romantic vision
of an Old and New Edinburgh of hills and monuments, and the
religio-capitalistic energy of imperial Glasgow. The Modernist Age
gave a more precise focus to the idea of the city region and its
problems. Geddes coined the generic term 'conurbation' and proposed its specific application to the Central Belt, under the unifying heading of 'Clydeforth'; and his emphasis on the importance
of survey, in contrast to radical surgical intervention, made clear
the possibility of constructing a psychic geography of the conurbation, reshaping it selectively around what already exists. That
cumulative heritage, as we saw above, now also includes the
large-scale Modernist plans which followed Geddes, with their
attempts to order entire city regions – although not yet the Central
Belt conurbation as a whole – and plant new communities in open
landscape. And it also includes the consequences of the conservation movement and the Postmodern period, in which the balance
tilted further towards the old, rather than the new, as the main
ordering factor.

In the past decade, among younger architects and commentators
on the Scottish urban environment, a range of opinions has
begun to emerge as to how we can shape a new modernity rooted
in the power of the city as narrative. All of them attribute a basic
ordering power to what already exists, but draw very different
conclusions from it. One key element in that change has been the
growth of the phenomenological and psychic emphasis on the direct

experience of buildings' substance and of space. This allows the cumulative evolution of the urban fabric to take on its own autonomous life and validity. Originally associated with the Modernist idea of empathy in architectural form and space, invented around a century ago in Germany, this concept has become increasingly bound up with a rejection of Utopian or Cartesian ideas of planned order, and an emphasis on the *genius loci* of the city. Elements of 'likeness' and 'reflection' are balanced with 'difference' and 'contrast', steering between the opposing reefs of 'contextual' pastiche and wilful posturing in an attempt to reconcile modern freedom with the cumulative authority of the narrative city – including a reinterpretation of the recent chapters of that narrative represented by the Modern Movement.

Let us see, now, how far this Eutopian formula of regeneration of the existing spatial fabric can be extended to the scale of the conurbation, and can be employed to address our own problems of Clydeforth. Then, in the next two chapters, we can focus more closely on the reform of the components of the conurbation: its towns and cities.

TAMING THE CONURBATION

Conurbations or city regions, across the world, are organised in two main ways: in a truly polycentric form, as in the case of Los Angeles or the Randstad; or in the more hierarchical form of the great city with extensive suburbs, such as New York or London. What is common to all conurbations, even their defining characteristic, is their vast expanse of amorphous semi-urban territory. Two key problems flow from the latter: its relationship to the existing centres within it, and its relationship to the landscape outside. The conurbation is different in scale and significance from the suburb, whose status is defined in its name. In a polycentric conurbation containing pre-existing cities embedded within it, both the old centres and their suburbs are equal in standing. In this vast territory, everything is in flux and everything is up for grabs. The resulting overlap of the problems of urban design and regional strategy is highlighted by *Europan* head Didier Rebois:

> as we witness the end of the dependence of peripheral areas upon town centres, and their emancipation to form constellation towns, the subject for discussion is the multiple development of these new urban territories, jigsaw towns combining infrastructure networks, micro-centralities, hybrid spaces, autonomous fragments and abandoned spaces.[38]

The central concern of the city of the past was to give order to the impulses of openness and freedom. For us, today, the challenge of the conurbation is even wider and less tractable. Faced with this, it is all too easy for the designer to yield to escapism, to lavish care on the creation of individual, jewelled masterpieces of form. And it becomes all the more difficult to insist on engagement with the city, in a context where even the legitimacy of collective intellectual solutions is fundamentally in question. Owing to the decline of teleological Progress and the state's intervention powers, any civic and public structuring element has to be selective and judicious, rather than sweepingly aggressive. Yet engagement is all the more vital here for that very reason. We have to try to construct reform on the sum total of the conurbation that already exists – on the established old towns, the new neighbourhoods of the twentieth century, and the landscape around and in between. This task, of building on urban and regional *genius loci*, is one which the early and mid- twentieth century would probably have understood as one of 'planning'. It was a task which the Modernist Utopian architect-planners were not afraid to tackle with synthesising boldness. We today no longer share their driving zeal, yet a vision based on ideal and actual place is also an inescapable necessity for us.

What kind of actual conurbation are we dealing with? In contrast to megacities such Berlin, Beijing or Moscow, spreading across a featureless plain, or the artificially constructed urban topography of the Dutch Randstad, our own specific conurbation of the Central Belt enjoys a number of clear advantages of differentiation, both externally and internally. Externally, it is highly defined by landscape, in the form of both hills and water. Seen from within the urban areas of the conurbation, the landscape is defined chiefly by the overall east-west alignment of the two firths, Forth and Clyde, and by their bounding lines of hills to north and south. This linear grouping is ruptured by the major intrusion of the north-south upland watershed at its centre, an interruption which makes us aware of the rural expanses that lie beyond, as well as the more isolated urban centres outwith the Central Belt, such as Dundee and Aberdeen: we could almost talk of an intersecting east-west urban axis and north-south rural axis. The built-environment issues of the latter are quite different from those of the centre, and in no case amount to a systemic conurbation crisis. A stand-alone city such as Aberdeen enjoys a clear relation with its hinterland, while in the Highlands and other rural areas, the built environment is arguably one of the most insignificant worries, in comparison with the wider problems of economy, society and landscape.

The frame of reference of this book is defined above all by the east-west urban axis. In this context, the landscape is seen not as a rural environment in its own right, but as the external definition, or outer rim, of the conurbation. Our proposal is that this external border should be reconceived, to make it far harder-edged. Modernist regional planning tried to draw a sharp border around settlements within the conurbation. Those edges were formed by protected green belts – a policy which, as we will see shortly, has now lost its original meaning and should be reassessed. In our view, the green belt should now be displaced outwards, to become a new outer edge of the whole conurbation, formed naturally by the ranges of hills running to the north and south of it, and by the central watershed. In some places, that edge is very close to the existing big towns: for example, south of Greenock or Edinburgh.

Thus, the external definition of this conurbation is largely straightforward. A far greater challenge comes from its internal structure. This can be summarised as a generally polycentric network of towns, focused on the bipolar city relationship of Glasgow and Edinburgh, and with numerous subsidiary pre- and post-industrial centres and twentieth-century new towns dotted around. It is, in effect, a half-way house between the completely decentred or polycentric and the strongly hierarchical types of conurbation. This structure has all the problems of polarisation and fragmentation of the generic Postmodern conurbation, including the problem of the relationship, and relative importance, of centres and background. Should that background, whether urban sprawl or green belt, largely be left to its own devices? The present green belt freezes from development whatever land around the cities happened to be undeveloped in the 1940s; but it takes no positive steps to enhance or protect that land. The result is a blight on the general conurbation environment, whose pervasive but slow-acting effects echo, in a curious way, the earlier impact of the 1915 rent controls on the private-rented housing stock. This insidious process of disintegration can be seen, for example, south-east of Edinburgh and north-east of Glasgow: a no-man's land of decay, with crumbling walls, torn-up trees, rubbish everywhere. The present green belt is a vacuum which (in the absence of active planning) actively draws in the market-led parcellisation and development pressures of Clone City.

The east-west contrast, which forms the Central Belt's main internal cultural tension, has also become diverted into a highly unhealthy form of destructive competition. Cultural-architectural contests, such as that concerning the 1999 Year of Architecture festival or the National Gallery of Scottish Art, have pitted rival slogans and caricatures against one another: demotic Glasgow triumphalism versus snobbish Edinburgh elitism. In these short-sighted culture wars, Glasgow has up to now been the more successful. But the coming establishment of the new Scottish government and parliament in Edinburgh, a city already bursting with festivals and tourists all year round, must increasingly raise the possibility of an eastwards migration of cultural and political institutions after the turn of the century, exploiting the prestige of the parliament as well as the massive hidden subsidies which support the capital's many 'national' cultural attractions, to the point where Edinburgh's population may even eventually outstrip that of Glasgow – an outcome significant less in its own right than as an indication of the zero-sum character of the two cities' rivalry. In competition, they can only damage each other and the nation, but together, they can add up to a tremendous creative force.

The contrasting cultures of east and west first emerged in a complementary relationship to each other, and now they need to be brought back together into a common, cooperative framework. To achieve that synthesis, we need not just statements of friendship and good intention, but a common vision. Today's unrestrained conflict between Glasgow and Edinburgh, a conflict of images and masks, is a classic example of Clone City's disintegrative tendencies, of globalist freedom running uncontrolled. It must be regulated, and synthesised into a more ordered framework, but in a way which takes account of the modern, periphery-driven realities of those two cities today. Fundamentalist calls for a return to the old, dense centres are simply irrelevant.

As we saw in Chapter 2, Geddes's vision apprehended the Central Belt not in the obvious terms of east and west groupings, but as one conurbation, 'Clydeforth', a loosely arranged organism which, in his view, required sensitive clarification and enrichment through the ethically informed framework of civic planning, to bring together and creatively synthesise the eastern and western cultural traditions. He argued that Clydeforth was a 'city group' composed of specialised and complementary elements, which in combination could aspire to first-rank status: 'we have to prepare for a great and living city . . . which would be second to none.'[37] Today, of course, the actual specialisations Geddes proposed for west and east – imperial heavy industry versus elite civic culture – are now obsolete. But what is still as important as ever is the principle that the east and west are complementary, that they are two halves of a whole, and that the creative energy potentially unleashed by their combination can be of not only national but even international status: on Geddes's scale, in economic as well

Central Leith

John Smith & Son
BOOKSHOPS
57 St Vincent Street
Glasgow G2 5TB
Scotland
TEL: 0141-221 7472
FAX: 0141-248 4412
email: 57@johnsmith.co.uk
http://www.johnsmith.co.uk
Vat Reg No. GB259 5488 08

DATE: 31/05/1999 TIME: 17:01
TILL: 0004   NO: 04040033
CASHIER: ANGELA L

DESCRIPTION	QTY	AMOUNT
Barcode: 9780748662555		
CLONE CITY :,GLENDIN	1	11.99 A
TOTAL	1	£11.99
BOOK TOKEN CREDIT		£1.00
BOOK TOKEN CREDIT		£1.00
BOOK TOKEN CREDIT		£20.00
JS Credit Issued		£10.01

VAT A @ 0.00% (£11.99): £0.00

Thank you for visiting our Bookshop.
We look forward to seeing you again
in our General Books Department.
OPENING HOURS:
Monday-Saturday: 9.00am until 6.00pm
Sunday: 12.00pm until 4.00pm
LATE NIGHT THURSDAY: 7.00pm

A SCOTTISH BOOKSHOP
FOUNDED IN GLASGOW IN 1751

JOHN SMITH & SON

BOOKSHOPS

founded in Glasgow in 1751.
The oldest continuously trading
independent bookseller in the
English speaking world.

Visit our Website at:
http://www.johnsmith.co.uk

Thank you for visiting
John Smith & Son Bookshops

JOHN SMITH & SON

BOOKSHOPS

founded in Glasgow in 1751.
The oldest continuously trading
independent bookseller in the

Central Dumbarton

as in cultural terms, the current aspiration of the Glasgow Development Agency for 'second-rank European city' status seems timid indeed! Once the conurbation principle is conceded, and Clydeforth's complex of problems is accepted as *the* national challenge of urban regeneration – in parallel with the issues of rural and Highland revival – then it becomes possible to conceive of radical solutions that can override existing demarcations within the conurbation.

Such a synthesising vision proved to be beyond even the Modernist planners of the mid-twentieth century. But what they achieved has nonetheless largely shaped our problems and opportunities today. They developed the idea of conurbation planning in divergent ways, west and east, the two being treated as self-contained regions. The vast plan of decentralisation proposed by Patrick Abercrombie and Robert Matthew in the west, including completely new towns of 50,000–100,000 inhabitants, set out to convert Clydeside into a constellation-like urban structure during a forty-year period of population outmigration from Glasgow. It established the principle that municipal power and boundaries were not sacrosanct, but could be overridden in the wider national interest. But this victory left in its wake vast and unresolved demographic-economic tensions and spatial scars. The east was addressed by the more modest vision of Geddes's son-in-law, Frank Mears, of medium-scaled settlements of 10,000–15,000 people, consolidating and regenerating existing nuclei rather than abandoning and starting anew, with Edinburgh itself left almost intact.

Now, what seems to be beginning is a reversal of the old economic and population pressure patterns of the Central Belt. Overheated Edinburgh is replacing overcrowded Glasgow as the focus of congestion, while Glasgow is experiencing problems of depopulation and emptiness. The most effective response to this mounting crisis is not simply to grab for today's simplistic architectural slogan of the 'dense city', nor on the other hand to throw up one's hands and surrender to the anarchy of Clone City. Rather, the time has finally arrived to revisit in earnest the unifying framework of Clydeforth, by drawing on all the planning experiences we have accrued up to now, and synthesising their lessons into a new vision of, and for, the Central Belt: a vision which combines an overall unity with the maximum internal differentiation.

The Scottish heritage of urban planning has bequeathed us two main ways of combining urban foci and lower-density background development, two ways that up to now have roughly corresponded to east and west. On the one hand, there is the focal city-planning formula devised in Edinburgh and the east, with its intensely designed, tightly coordinated balance of an Old Town and setting. Here the pre-modern era showed how to create an embedded historic core juxtaposed with new, unified developments and dramatic natural landscape, so as to form a single unity rooted in the past. And the twentieth-century Modernist work of Mears, Frank Tindall and Wheeler & Sproson demonstrated how decayed smaller towns could be regenerated in the same way. On the other hand, there is the more dynamic, open city-planning formula which was pioneered especially in nineteenth- and twentieth-century Glasgow and the west. This showed how a looser framework of commercial and industrial zones, and residential suburbs, could be evolved first on a city scale, then on a regional scale, creating a flexible, open urban network suitable for the twenty-first century.

The time is now ripe for a strategy of open, place-sensitive decentralisation for Clydeforth as a whole, a strategy driven by the fact that the problems of east and west are complementary. Rather than two regional visions separated by a *cordon sanitaire*, we have to begin to think in terms of a single, linear city belt, defined by the landscape cross of the north-south watershed and west-east firths – a constellation comprising two major clusters: one around the Forth, one around the Clyde. Its overall ordering framework is that of a consolidation and cross-fertilisation of the existing focal and open frameworks in east and west. In some ways, this represents a looser development of the Modernist zoning concept, extending now to the specialisation of whole cities rather than just districts. In the east, the tradition of focal planning

Linlithgow

Grangemouth

can be reinvigorated, and the pressures of growth countered, by a strong injection of decentralisation planning from the Clyde Valley tradition, defending the external definition of Edinburgh and diverting population to other towns in the Lothians and Fife. In Glasgow and the west, the ragged ends left by the open-planning framework can be tackled in a way which partly continues the Clyde Valley Plan dispersal principle, but which combines this with more closely controlled, embedded foci on the pattern pioneered by Edinburgh, coalescing around both a more tightly defined Glasgow and new groupings formed out of the surrounding old and new towns. The order and integrity of urban settlement in its landscape roots can now be extended from the 'old' east to the 'new' west, while the outward-flowing freedom and spatial generosity of Modern regional planning can be applied to the east, and to Clydeforth as a whole.

This model of cross-fertilisation of east and west is inspired, in particular, by the general planning principle of the postwar new towns. We will return later to focus on the specific ways in which the new towns can help in our restructuring of areas of exurban sprawl. Here, we are concerned with the way in which the new town, generically, could almost stand as a microcosm for the whole of Clydeforth: for almost all the five new towns were built around embedded old towns or villages, tied together with new housing zones by careful landscaping and all contained within a sharp-edged juxtaposition with the rural environment, and controlled by one overall vision. Clydeforth, reimagined and reshaped, will be not a new town but a 'new conurbation', with specialised cities and regions, rather than specialised zoned neighbourhoods.

But simply devising a new conceptual model, however all-embracing and sophisticated, will not, in itself, alter or stem economic or population flows or spatial imbalances. After all, vast Utopian remodelling schemes are no longer organisationally possible, with the withdrawal of the state from mass provision across Europe. Even in the highly planned Netherlands, the current national land-use plan (*VINEX*) assumes that private-enterprise provision will dominate in the future. And grand schemes are also ideologically unacceptable, now that the use-value (*Gebrauchswert*) principle has been extended from the pre-Modernist heritage environments to the entire built environment of modernity, right up to the point of today's breakdown of order. There must also be, alongside our high aspirations, a restraining modesty of expectation. Where the New Towns were built up on a huge scale using vast state powers and spending, the building of Clydeforth will require a much more selective process, of adjustment and clarification of messy spots and grey areas between existing foci – a pattern closest, among all New Towns, to the Mears-like complexity of Glenrothes and Irvine. On the one hand, there is a general continuity of 'fabric', without glaring gashes; but on the other, a high degree of variety within the structure.

Yet to make Clydeforth something real, rather than an abstraction confined to the realms of Geddesian rhetoric, will require something more than just patching and infilling, more active strategies of tying together its two halves, new physical and metaphorical lines of force to make real the linear conurbation. That requirement of psychic geography increasingly now coincides with the practical demand for improved public transport. Only through radically improved rail links, in particular, will it be possible to extend our formula of highly differentiated focal centres in planned space from the scale of a town to that of a conurbation. Where the uncontrolled public subsidisation of developer sprawl by new road scheme investments has atomised the city, the enhancement of fast public transport can allow us to balance mobility with the cultural authority of the old urban nuclei. The task of curbing the use of the private car and revitalising public transport is not only a matter of vehicles and fares, but also a rich potential area of architectural ennoblement of the collective urban life. That potential is demonstrated in countless schemes of coordinated transport infrastructure within cities on the Continent, or, nearer at hand, in the civic ambition of the Tyne-Wear Metro programme in northern England. And an even more elevated architecture of the collective is expressed in the infrastructure of high-speed public-transport links between cities, of soaring station canopies and viaducts tying the nation together with grandeur and dignity.

What would be the effect, for example, of the construction of a 300 kph high-speed rail line from Edinburgh to Glasgow Airport and on to Prestwick? It is perhaps no coincidence that, at this time of simmering east-west hostility, the Glasgow–Edinburgh rail journey today is slower than it was in 1971. If the rail journey across the Central Belt were to become no longer than a twenty-minute bus trip across central Edinburgh, the national institutions of Scotland could be shared across Clydeforth as if within a single city. At that point the culture and investment wars between east and west would become not only meaningless, but also impossible – like a fight between left and right arms.

Up to now, the financial and organisational means to allow projects such as this are still lacking, and their development is not yet certain. As illustrated by the controversy-dogged attempts to implement the Clyde Valley Plan in the 1940s–1960s, in the face of opposition from many in Glasgow, the charting out of long-term strategies is an inherently uncertain matter. For the present, we can only deal with the geography of the Central Belt as it is, and as it might be in the immediate future. In the next chapter, our focus narrows from the general external and internal definition of Clydeforth to the reshaping of its components. Can we apply, at this scale, the same principle of cross-fertilisation of the eastern focal-city and western open-city traditions?

Glasgow Central Station

Wemyss Bay Station

5
CENTRES OF LIFE
Eutopian Cities of Tomorrow

At the level of the individual Scottish city or community, the relationship between focal and open planning is a rolling conflict which is forever redefined in the light of cultural change. It reflects the tension between the private and individual on the one hand, and the public and collective on the other. Clone City today has given up any intellectual and spatial integrity in that relationship. There is a polarisation between a rhetoric of continuous fabric and traditional city, and a reality of rampant market fragmentation, whether in inner heritage zones or outer sprawl. The task facing us is that of establishing a renewed integrity, which will reflect today's variegated society in its diverse solutions.

The tradition of the Scottish planned city since the Age of Improvement has always tried to control change and spread through a very strong spatial order, both in its internal arrangement and in its hierarchy of building types. The early capitalist city in Scotland, unlike the by then old-fashioned muddle of uses and social classes of the Continental city, was increasingly differentiated and divided out, with parcelled-out suburbs, business areas, parks and industrial areas, and a growing emphasis on the creation of space and separation. In the long streets of new self-contained dwellings, whether tenements or terraced houses, the definition of a category of background building of high finish but muted architecture was established: not every building could be special. This framework was also quite hierarchical, and there were limits to the combination of focal and open. Its most carefully demarcated relationships of spaces and solids were largely reserved for the wealthy, with relatively undifferentiated space left over for the poor. Even the most open frameworks, such as those of the western suburbs of Glasgow, were still highly controlled, with sharp juxtapositions of hard ashlar stone or iron with trees.

Under the Modern Movement, in reaction against all this, the public and private spheres were extended to all, and balanced spatially. This egalitarian fusion was symbolised by the mass building of self-contained dwellings with flowing open space all around, and the redevelopment of vast city areas and the building of complete new towns on segregated, zoned lines – the synthesising element being the New. But these attempts to integrate the extremes of openness and segregation tore apart the industrial cities, and in reaction, Postmodernists attempted to reassert more organically mixed, 'traditional' city patterns. Many of these had actually begun as dissenting elements within the Modern Movement, with accompanying organic metaphorical language of 'grain', 'carpet', 'spine'. Under Postmodernism, they were changed into fundamentalist images which served to conceal the fragmented reality of urban change in Clone City.

So now we are in a state of multiple alienation, separated as if by a curtain from any kind of urban reality, whether pre-Modernist, Modernist or Postmodern. That curtain is the vision of the city as an ideally seamless unity, with each new intervention seen as an insertion into a context rather than as a freestanding 'object'. Extending the metaphors, the city is a fabric, in which 'tears' must be 'mended' or 'knitted together' – in conscious opposition to the Modernist Utopian visions of objects set in continuous space. This fundamentalist ideal is based on a medievalising ideal of the pedestrian, enclosed old town, and especially on the Morrisian interpretation of conservation, with its proliferation of sacrosanct old urban fabric. It is an ideal focused especially on the city centres, the smaller historic towns and parts of inner heritage suburbs. In its most intransigent form, it disregards not only the reality of what is happening today, but also the lessons of what went before. These included Modern Movement open city concepts, ordered by functional zoning, as well as the earlier lessons of eighteenth- and nineteenth-century Edinburgh, in which controlled vistas were vitally dependent on open spaces

Craigshill, Livingston New Town

and landscapes brought into the heart of the city, and the unity was a unity of diversity rather than of just one 'mixed', 'dense' recipe.

The Eutopian framework of pragmatic change offers a striking alternative to this fundamentalist imagery. It combines the weight and authority of what exists, with the freedom and openness stemming from change; it continues and combines both the focal and open city visions. For urban change is still in full flood. We cannot pretend that the iron bonds of family, industrial class community or unitary nation still remain, when they have so obviously been ripped apart. In every aspect of the modern Scottish city and built environment – in its disposition of space and intensity of development, in its degree of order, in its choice of building type – new and complex realities are continuing to force themselves into the open. That is as true at the micro-level, of the individual city district or even building, as it is at the level of the conurbation.

In a great city-centre public building it is now hardly possible to insist on a traditional stately self-containment. The lessons of free plan and section, their potential for freedom within the collective, subvert any attempt at a pre-Modern hierarchical dignity, despite the continuing Postmodernist cry for 'traditional' facades in the city. That dissolution has been most recently, and brilliantly, exploited in Benson & Forsyth's new Museum of Scotland. And in the individual home, little-box thinking is also developing internal conflicts. The clone home is beginning to transform itself, bursting out from its straitjackets of cottage roof or tenement wall, dissolving interior and exterior space to symbolise the new variety in lifestyles. This gradual change is visible even in speculative suburbia, where the supposedly conservative taste of Scottish households is disintegrating from within. There is a growing disparity between the industrially prepackaged variety of house exteriors and the unstructured freedom inside.

Everywhere, the germs of a new urban spatial structure are visible, one which expresses the conflicting demands of today by

Wester Coates Estate, Edinburgh

balancing the open and focal city visions. Our task is to build on those foundations: to respond to the mounting crisis of household formation, while remembering that the new households are themselves created by individuality and freedom; to acknowledge the popularity of our dense old towns, and the need to curb the divisive 'choice' represented by car-fuelled sprawl, while respecting the liberating power of the Modernist vision of space and mobility, especially for the disadvantaged; to recover or fashion the sense of hierarchy and specialisation necessary in great cities, including a proper status for the residential suburb, and a proper scale and height nearer the centre; to balance the implications of popular heritage controls and organic urbanism with the boldly differentiated planning of the Modern new town vision.

To achieve these balances, there needs to be a coherent relationship between the whole and its various constituent parts. During the Historicist Age, visions of the City on a Hill tried to achieve this balance through the long-established hierarchy of stateliness, and through a pyramidal structure of urban intensity. Now, we have a more complex task of achieving a functional and physical differentiation of urban social groupings, to prevent everything being polarised between the simplistic formula of inner enclosure and the reality of outer sprawl. Today, as we saw in Chapter 3, the needs of individuals for freedom to realise their own potential have become far more complex. These needs include individual choice, of user involvement in the shaping of environments, of mobility for all, between and within cities. One person's restriction may be another's emancipation. For example, the restrictions on car use, needed to allow full realisation of enhanced public-transport systems, may actively assist the mobility of non-car users. And there is an almost limitless variety and potential coexistence of physical solutions to general strategic tasks. For example, in the relationship of open space to residential buildings, solutions range from the generalised, externalised space of Modernism – suitably clarified and structured for today's requirements – to the intensely internalised space concepts already pioneered

in some overseas housing projects of the 1990s, such as the dockland redevelopments in Amsterdam.

The almost incredible fluidity and difficulty of defining solutions
today is highlighted by the transformation in meaning of one key
word in debates about urban structure: 'density'. In the Modern
Movement period, it was used as a rationalistic way of summaris-
ing and systematising all these choices and permutations, as well
as relating different parts of a city to each other in terms of intensity of development. Through the shorthand of density figures,
expressed in persons per acre (ppa) in residential areas, and more
complicated calculations of plot ratio in central commercial zones,
different building types and area layouts could be compared and
assessed by simple thumbnail rules, in their relation to the scientific dogmas of Modernist planning, concerning daylight, sunlight,
open space provision and so forth. Under the Modern Movement,
density meant variety and differentiation – although these were
defined through a rationalistic method alien to us today.

To today's ideologists, the significance of density is quite different. It has been transformed into a metaphoric rather than a
factual matter, and, as we have seen, unbalanced in one direction –
towards a fundamentalist and Postmodernist interpretation of
the focal city. The association of rising housing demand with ever
smaller households has undermined the assumed relationship,
on any given site, between stacking of dwellings and density of
people, and has made meaningless the old scientific calculations.
Few architects are expected to 'know the density' of their project
any more. That is not to say, of course, that many of the individual
land-use restrictions that contributed to the old density compu-
tations, such as road widths and car-parking requirements, have
not survived. But these technical stipulations have been cast free
to proliferate in their own right. At the same time, architectural
density has become transformed into a psychic perception of
solid and space, linked by growing numbers of commentators to
a demand for higher density, and an admiration for authoritarian
or fundamentalist slogans such as the 'dense traditional city' or

(much less frequently in Scotland) the 'futurist skyscraper mega-city'. This fragmentation of the idea of density into technical and intuitive elements has powerfully fuelled the cause of Clone City. The homogeneity of the new image of the dense city undermines the potential for differentiated frameworks of urban and conurbation structure, and its divisiveness prompts an intellectual evacuation of the less dense peripheral areas.

In addressing this problem with a balanced formula which can feed into a wider conurbation vision, it is necessary to return to the idea of the city as a whole, to the cumulative authority of the city as a narrative. Here we are talking not of images, but of the actual substance of the city, including both the Historicist Age's radially ordered intensity of development, diminishing outwards from the centre towards the suburbs, and the dynamic and sometimes disruptive interventions of the Modernist Age. The contrasting elements contained within this substance point the way towards a fusion of integrity and modern openness, a framework depending on contrast and differentiation as much as on context and mixture, and esteeming the Modernist and pre-Modernist concepts of free space and tall buildings as a vital counterpoint to supposedly traditional enclosed space.

The general shape of our cities may have developed in response to violently conflicting principles, but the result is a complex and organic whole. No part of it, however unfashionable, can be cut out without wounding the whole body. In many ways the most vital, because least appreciated, potential ingredients in the open city of the future are the functionally differentiated Modernist environments, whether in inner redevelopment areas or in the peripheries and New Towns. Suitably reorganised to intensify and enrich the amorphous aspects of space that we reject today, these areas, with their unique combination of collective monumentality and openness, could provide both precious lungs of freedom and contact with nature in the inner city, and 'menhirs' of civic coherence in the periphery. Contrary to what is implied in the demagogic calls for mass demolition of tower blocks, these are not assets to be discarded lightly.

Gifford, East Lothian

BROWN BELTS AND GREEN CENTRES

If we look at the city through Eutopian spectacles, viewing it as a cumulative narrative in its own right, the structure of that built narrative is partly a literal matter of chronological topography, and partly metaphorical and psychic. The form of the narrative has been made much more complicated by the pervasive effects of the Modernist planning interventions. Rather than the simple radial pyramid of the nineteenth-century city or of today's Postmodern fundamentalist images of the 'traditional city', the various components of Clydeforth, like the conurbation as a whole, are composed of a much more complex balance of focal and background areas. The physical urban landscape still gradually opens out from enclosed and formal grandeur to more greenery and space, but cities and towns can now comprise single or multiple centres, surrounded by a more general public framework of collective arteries and open areas, and interspersed by ever larger, more easy-going spaces of private freedom.

This general framework is qualified throughout by the principle of *genius loci*, in its relation of new buildings and landscaping both to the natural setting of hills or water and to the existing built fabric, and in the emphasis on the distinctiveness of each area of the city in functional as well as visual terms. In general, the gradation from dense urbanity to greenery is most pronounced on the north and south edges of Clydeforth, where its borders are most tightly constrained by the hills and firths. But there is the potential for countless more specific distinctions. Whether we are talking about places where differentiation is obvious, such as the two halves of the old centre of Edinburgh, or places where it is urgently needed but is denied by Clone City, such as within or between Glasgow peripheral housing schemes, the governing principle is the same: the Eutopian Scottish city of the future cannot be assembled out of an identikit formula, whether of dense urban villages or of car-accessible exurban enclaves.

If this Eutopian conception of order in the Scottish city respects *genius loci* and the existing fabric, it must equally accommodate

Glasgow Inner Ring Road

demands for change. Of these, by far the most immediate and pressing is the seismic demographic shift away from the 'standard family' to smaller and more variegated households, something which is predicted to add 250,000 household units to housing need in the next decade: roughly six times the maximum annual output of new dwellings at the peak of the 1960s housing boom. This is closely bound up with the widely discussed crisis of urban transport, caused by the rapid growth in car ownership and the failure to counteract that growth by attractive and coordinated public transport. This demographic and locational crisis is part of an international trend across much of Western Europe. A similar demand is predicted under the Dutch *VINEX* plan, and a slightly higher level in England. The housing drive in post-reunification Germany, by contrast, has been of a more old-fashioned kind, coping with population growth and family demand. Previously, new Scottish social housing had been rationed by waiting lists under various subcategories (overcrowding, slum clearance, etc.), but now the more dramatic overall heading of 'homelessness' is used as a label for much social housing demand. This is said to have risen by two-thirds in the decade to 1996; the waiting list in Edinburgh was 24,000 in 1997, compared with only 6,000 in 1958. What has strongly declined in scale, but increased in prominence, compared with even the 1970s, is the problem of rooflessness, or destitution on the streets.

This demographic time bomb seems likely to return us, for the first time since the 1960s, to quantity-dominated housing policies and a consequent land-supply crisis. The question of land use is clearly a fundamental building block in the renewal both of planning mechanisms and of urban spatial structure. The end-lessly rehearsed rival solutions to this question focus on the use of either new greenfield sites outside towns (a policy backed especially by the house-building industry) or reused brownfield sites largely within towns (backed by conservationists and many rural inhabitants). Advocates of each solution claim the other will cost more (the brownfield in land rehabilitation costs, the green-field through infrastructure and transport costs) and will be more socially divisive. Between 1980 and 1994, brownfield sites provided over half of all private-sector housing land in Clydeside, often through large grants from the GDA and other public bodies. And the policy of even the previous Tory government gradually moved away from greenfield laissez-faire towards tighter controls.

Although some of the old passion for defending green belt stemmed from now outmoded wartime concerns of national agricultural self-sufficiency, in general it seems likely that the balance of policy will continue to move more and more emphatically towards brownfield policies. At the density proposed for a large, contemporary new-town development near Amsterdam (sixty dwellings per hectare) the currently registered derelict land in Scotland could accommodate the 250,000 required new dwellings more than three times over, and that within Glasgow alone could accommodate over 60,000 dwellings! If a brownfield-based strategy is pursued, the lessons of the density and space policies of the Modernist years will be of relevance, in pointing to ways of distributing the effects across the city. In inner areas, this could be achieved by carefully increasing the number of tall or dense buildings and abolishing the fixed requirement for car spaces and wide estate roads which have curbed the 'dwelling gain' to be obtained through their use. An increasingly dominant constraint on brownfield development is the high proportion of contaminated land, and the costs of treating it. Here, as we will see later, a policy of more sharply differentiated open space and buildings may also help offset these costs.

But what could most effectively enhance the brownfield formula, as suggested above, would be the replacement of the battered framework of the interurban green belt by a new outer green border, made up of the hills ringing Clydeforth as a whole, in combination with the establishment of a far more active system of landscape control for the interurban spaces. The existing green belt, with all its infills and contaminating elements, has now in effect become a kind of agricultural brownfield land, a 'brown belt' whose only remaining value to its owners is as a potential target for Clone City depradations. To counter that trend requires a bold response through a designed landscape strategy in conjunction with local-government redistributions, to avert the tide of tacky brickwork which is beginning to flow into vulnerable areas such as Easterhouse or south-east Edinburgh. The amorphous and neglected brown belt has to be reimagined as a necklace of green places, each with as much individuality and specific character as the parks within our older cities, or the green spaces within the postwar new towns, with their careful juxtaposition of landscaping with housing and industrial zones.

In the remainder of this chapter and the next, we deal with the problems of the inner city and the outer city – first in the abstract, and then in relation to the specific communities of Clydeforth – showing how today's damaging polarisation between the imagery of dense community and the reality of Clone City can be reconciled through a balance between traditional centres of gravity and new, more open formulae.

INNER CENTRES: TYRANNY OF THE TENEMENT

In the rhetoric of Postmodernism, the city centre, with its intensely developed concentration of stately public and commercial buildings, is the part of the city which is said to be least in need of clarification and regeneration. The 1980s saw a special emphasis on efforts to revitalise and reconceptualise the centre, whereas today the greatest challenges are claimed to lie outside it. But that contrast is in some ways a misleading one. Even in the city core there is, today, a lack of differentiation; a subtle, homogenising ossification.

Today, the assumed spatial norm of the centre city is a solid mass, out of which strictly demarcated spaces are excavated, in the conventionalised form of streets and squares. Yet while this formula reasserts a supposedly traditional relationship of solid and void in the aesthetic field, there is no return to the social realities associated with those spaces in the pre-Modern era. Mass secular rituals and political meetings mostly now take place in stadia and congress halls. Instead, the spaces are used in a

Livingston New Town

less ordered way, by a kind of new, aggregated, highly modern individual leisure consumption, modelled on tourism and often forming part of international city competition through commodified culture.

This is, in other words, another face of Clone City: the Image of Public Realm. It sits especially uncomfortably with the major public and commercial complexes which, after all, are the most prominent element in the city-centre environment. The result is often a polarisation between attempts to reassert the primacy of the traditional monumental civic or public building, and attempts to enlarge the irregular, contextual approach onto a grand scale. Compensating for the insistence on rigidly compartmentalised outside space is a growing preoccupation with fluidity of internal space, within the individual large building or street block. The freedom of Modernism has, in effect, been driven inside, and has been intensified. Often, the preserved facades of an old building are used as a shell for completely new interiors, relating to the city through such concepts as 'inhabited roofscape' and 'a building within a building'.

What has been edited out from this centre-city paradigm of dense fabric is the way in which spatial openness can be used to relieve the uniformity of unrelieved 'mixture'. The noblest Scottish inner-urban landscapes of the eighteenth and nineteenth centuries, after all, derive their general spatial and emotional effect from a pattern of free disposition of solid forms in continuous space, rather than from its supposedly traditional opposite, the enclosed space within a continuous fabric. That much is obvious from even a glance at the radical juxtapositions of the Edinburgh New and Old Towns with each other and with the dramatic landscapes around and in-between; or the liberal-capitalist openness of Glasgow's Blythswood new-town grid, with its relentlessly out-ward-marching streets and skyline. In contrast to these earlier paradigms, the relevance of the Modern Movement to the potential loosening up of the centre city is more problematic. During the postwar years, its strongest elements of spatial differentiation, including the vertical gestures of tower blocks, were applied only

Glenrothes New Town

cautiously to the established centres. As a result, most of the resulting spaces are of a half-finished, unstructured kind. This only accentuates the mask-like character of the fragments of new 'public realm' created more recently by Postmodernism alongside or within them. More recently, however, some master plans for central areas have begun to break from the homogeneity of the image of mixture, towards an acknowledgement of the potential of vertical differentiation.

The fundamentalism of the continuous-fabric metaphor also risks distorting the social reality of the centre city, through its assumption of the uniform applicability of the mixed-use formula. Of course, a concentration on cultural and public activities is a central aspect of modern centre-city existence. But the specialisation of life there has not yet vanished, with many commercial jobs still requiring face-to-face contact. Sectors other than the street-culture zones are often highly specific in their uses, especially for varieties of office, retail, warehouse and transport use. The inclusion of residential and private space, in the centre, has up to now normally been associated with relatively dense plans of the established mixed, street-block type, such as Elder & Cannon's 1980s designs for Glasgow's Ingram Square. However, the potential for a spatially and formally more varied solution, using higher blocks to break open free space in the fabric, offers a fruitful alternative.

This subtle spatial and social stagnation of the 'mixed' centre city is the result of a conflation of visual image and land use. It is agreed by all today that the governing formula of the centre must be one of respect for the existing totality, and change through conservative surgery. In Clone City's Image of Public Realm, that totality is defined as the literal, continuous fabric of mixed-use building, and nothing more. It is almost like a stage set. But in the Scottish city of the past and, hopefully, of the future, the totality is one not of image but of use. All space must be used, not left derelict or in ragged gap sites, but that use must be given a bold spatial differentiation.

154

Glasgow city centre

Clone City

In the areas which immediately ring the centres of Clydeforth's cities and large towns, the balance shifts sharply away from elite buildings towards the everyday environment. Yet the public or civic interest, the interest in collective regulation, is still just as vital here. Everyone passes through these areas en route to the centre. Here, the way of satisfying the civic impulse must be mostly by ennoblement of the ordinary, rather than design of the special. The dominant area of activity for these ambiguities is housing, especially social housing. Urban housing is the front line in the architectural battleground between the spatial and psychic worlds of the public/collective and the private/individual – an interaction which has become more confused with the decomposition of the once-rigid 'family'.

In this zone of ambiguity, there is more obvious opportunity than in the centres for a new and active vision. The extent of that opportunity, in any individual town, depends on the extent of slum clearance and reconstruction during the twentieth century. In pre-industrial towns with relatively little demolition, the task of the planner or architect is to develop small sites and spaces in response to their context, and that of the landscape architect is to revisualise the urban parks of the eighteenth and nineteenth centuries in a more diverse and specific way. In towns that were radically cleared, mainly nineteenth-century industrial centres, there is no need to to create openness, as it is there already in abundance, often in grotesque excess, through a combination of the residue of clearances, the effects of a new round of clearance of some Modernist areas, and the growing expense of land decontamination requirements. In these areas, unlike in the dense outer schemes, the task is generally to repopulate. In Glasgow's East End zone, for instance, the city council hope for a population increase of nearly 10 per cent between 1981 and 2001.

The architectural response to this challenge, just as in the centre, has been dominated by the fundamentalism of 'traditional' enclosed space and community. Most architectural commentators try to simplify, and give roots to, the many-sided challenge of urban housing by using 'the traditional tenement' as a benchmark

Edinburgh city centre

concept. Their conception of the Scottish city is that of a series of solids and voids, with the tenement facades as the outer faces of the densely packed solids. They argue that, around that spatial framework, the nineteenth century built an urban community of mixed use and mixed classes in the European manner. This nostalgic interpretation has its ultimate origin in the later Modernist and Postmodernist polemic against rigid zoning and open planning. Actually, pre-1914 Scottish urban housing, in its obsession with spatial openness, sanitary hygiene and public–private segregation, contrasted very strongly with the far denser tenement blocks of Continental *Mietskasernen* (rental barracks): the huge back courts of Scottish cities were unknown in Berlin or Vienna! In its concern with openness, pre-Modernist Scottish housing arguably had more in common with its Modernist Scottish successors than with its Continental contemporaries. But historical fact never stood in the way of a good myth. And since 1981, the myth of the dense tenement community, the cult of Tenementopia, has virtually monopolised architectural debate over Scottish urban housing.

Initially, the intellectual advocacy of Tenementopia was closely bound up with the mawkish 'stairheid nostalgia' of populist writers, but more recently it has drawn closer to the urban village ideology. Increasingly, the semi-cleared spaces of Glasgow and other heavily redeveloped Clydeside towns have attracted proposals to reconstruct the 'traditional city' by building a new grid of mixed-use streets across them. Glasgow commentators have prepared perspectives showing the cleared spaces of the East End of Glasgow 'restored' to dense mixed use, yet curiously sanitised by the omission of the smoke-belching factories that formed an essential part of the area as it actually was in the nineteenth century. Tradition, even in these once-industrial towns, is defined in terms of a pre-industrial, or even non-industrial, vision. At the same time, these backward-looking visions assume that enclosed space is the natural pattern for such areas, and that Modern openness must be expunged. Faced with evidence that inner-city residents value greenery and space as much as anyone else (as shown, for instance, in the bitter protests of Leith residents against the recent removal of a ragged gap site for a mixed-use redevelopment) the response is to structure that space into tightly demarcated public streets and squares, and private back areas – a pattern seen as applicable to any kind of city environment, except of course that of industry.

Seen through the distorting prism of Tenementopia, all other inner-urban debate, all change and evolution, is refracted and fragmented. Yet there are a number of disconnected but significant indications that, in housing, the ground is beginning to shift beneath our feet. With the collapse of the prestige and financial viability of state-managed mass housing, the authority of the standard housing solution has vanished as well. Every indication now points to the need for the specialised, the tailor-made, the diverse. Already, there are initiatives such as housing to cater for the special needs implications of the 1990 Community Care Act, and abroad there are more ambitiously innovative patterns, like the long-standing Scandinavian ideal of the *kollektivhus*, or today's experimental Dutch designs for new patterns of living, such as working from home or non-'nuclear family' cohabitation. The old Modernist practical and hygienic restraints on housing design and density, such as daylight and sunlight, building and lift costs, have been transformed by the shift to greater sustainability in design.

It is now possible to speak of the possibility and even the necessity for a break with the tenement – in certain circumstances. The key constraint is the strength of the existing context, whether we are talking of an infill or a largely new pattern on a large cleared site. In more or less built-up neighbourhoods of the industrial era, the tenement must remain a basic reference point. But alongside it, we should not forget another old urban type: the individual 'terraced' row house, or townhouse. This, in neighbouring Ireland, England, Denmark and the Low Countries, is the tenement's equivalent as the basic middle- and working-class dwelling, whereas in nineteenth-century Scotland it was a form used mainly for larger dwellings. Its plan form allows for flexible differences in function and height between different floors within one dwelling, and a generally more varied psychic framework of habitation. There is the possibility of a paradoxically somewhat denser exploitation of the individual plot, including a small private open space. The flexibility of this slotted-in model in catering for the new diverse types of households, rather than the old-fashioned 'standard family' assumed in much tenement rhetoric, should not be underestimated.

These nineteenth-century reference-point models, including the tenement and the row house, can also be modified almost indefinitely by the requirements of modern living. For example, there are the possibilities of innovations of plan, such as variable room sizes; or of breaking up elevations to explore the modern ambiguity between private and public, and undermine the image of the sharp wall division, allowing light in by day and light out by night. During the 1980s, there was growing awareness of the disparity in room heights between nineteenth- and twentieth-century housing, and calls for building in scale with the older tenements. Modernist devices of free sectional planning were put to the un-Modernist external task of differentiating between the front and back of dwellings, with taller, grander public rooms on one side, and lower storeys of private rooms on the other. Glasgow architectural academic Mark Baines designed a series of unexecuted, but influential split-level urban housing schemes combining elements of tenement and row house, and higher living rooms to the front. The same principle was echoed in a competition-winning classical block by McGurn, Logan, Duncan & Opfer with Ken MacRae (1984–8), and in several 1990s projects by Elder & Cannon and Simister & Monaghan.

While, on dense infill sites, the existing context of layout and scale is generally a pre-Modernist one, and the scope for variation between tenemental enclosed solutions and more open patterns is relatively narrow, the situation is very different on sites where a large amount of cleared or open space is available. There, the policy of using new tenements to 'recreate mixed community', far from reasserting *genius loci*, actually undermines it. It confronts

Pollokshields, Glasgow

us with the question of the legitimacy of Modernist open-planning, and especially of the role of the tower block in rupturing traditional space. It is especially in the former industrial towns of Clydeside and in Glasgow that there are large inner redeveloped areas dotted with tower blocks.

Should we continue to label tower blocks as a bad thing, and try to break up Modernist open space by all possible means – including the 'execution' of towers as a public spectacle? Or should we begin to take a positive view of this legacy, bearing in mind that the opinions of those who actually live in multi-storey flats are usually far less negative than those of usual public perception? Whereas new tower blocks in the 1960s were indiscriminately used to rehouse large numbers of families with children, today the situation is radically different, in the context of a demographic explosion overwhelmingly comprising single-person households.[39] These are precisely the people most suited to high living: people who want the freedom to live their lives without having the lifestyle of the standard family with children forced on them. That claim is not a speculative one, but is firmly grounded in the actual experience of the city of Aberdeen. Not only did the Granite City's meticulously managed multi-storey programme meet with none of the problems common in the Central Belt, but it was followed, in the late 1970s and 1980s, by an exceptionally popular series of sheltered-housing tower blocks for older citizens, who value their combination of privacy and collective life. We in the Central Belt can learn much from Aberdeen's experience. Tower blocks, once unloved relics of the postwar social housing boom of disciplined 'mass', are now potential beacons of the social freedom that has followed the bursting open of the iron cage of family values. Just as the successful completion of urban hygienic reconstruction allowed the revival of the tenement in the 1970s, so now, with the collapse of the disciplined community of family and fertility, the time has arrived for an urgent reassessment of the possibilities of high flats for the furthering of community with privacy in the Scottish city.

Greenock

Clone City

At the outset, it is worth suggesting some general guiding principles of a revival of the high block. Any new tower designs, in their public aspects, should follow the gap site locational principle followed by many 1960s blocks, rather than the huge comprehensive redevelopments beloved of the architectural and planning establishment of the time. On the whole, they should be used in the denser, inner zones of the city, especially in the form of isolated landmark blocks. What is not acceptable today is to build phalanxes of towers and slabs, especially in inaccessible locations. In their architectural aspects, they should be designed in a manner which attempts to respond creatively and individually to the spatial and psychic aspects of the Scottish urban *genius loci*. The Modernist era is rich in precedents for such an approach, including the stone- and timber-clad towers added by Robert Matthew to Dundee and Edinburgh Universities; or the lower and more irregular types of freely planned Modern redevelopment in smaller towns, such as Wheeler & Sproson's Dysart redevelopment, with its mini-towers, as well as countless other modest, plain, rendered, informal schemes in smaller burghs.

The challenge of the Scottish inner-urban community of the future is to combine complexity and access to local commercial and social facilities with a degree of openness and specialisation – including a revival in the idea of the separate residential area. Taking a selective and sensitive look at our Modernist inner-redevelopment heritage, with its fluid use of concrete and render, might even allow us to find a way out of the present pernicious association between the 'traditional tenement' and that most untraditional material in the Scottish city, brightly coloured brickwork. That association perhaps harks back unconsciously to the mid-nineteenth-century insistence on high-finish ashlar rather than rough harl or rubble, a preference rejected as tasteless by the turn-of-century arts and crafts reformers, but now perversely resurrected, in brick form, as a diktat of some city planning officials.

IN-BETWEEN CENTRES:
CHAOS OF THE CUL-DE-SAC

Whereas the inner city is subject to a more subtle, orderly desta-
bilisation by Postmodernism, through the advocacy of 'restoration'
of a uniform tenemental fabric, in the outer zone, the heart of
the area of private freedom, the problem is very different: one
of complete fragmentation. Here the mixed community or urban
village theme is more tenuous, being applied in the form of atomised, car-borne enclaves. The reality is one of an overall extreme
of unstructured openness, combined with subdivisions of the
most minute and disorientating kind.

In reasserting any kind of environmental integrity in this elusive
setting, general framework or master-planning controls over development form and building material constitute the first building
block – to ensure that even at low density, even in the least prestigious, most everyday places, we can aspire to some kind of ideal
of integrity which responds to our past legacy of city planning,
from the Edinburgh New Town to the post-1945 New Towns. But
in planning for today, we have to plan in response not to the constraints of those past eras, but to today's concepts of the balance
between freedom and order, private and public. Our aspiration
must be to synthesise flowing, landscaped space and greenery
with the armature of spatial intensity and specialisation demanded
by the present day. Just as in the overall definition of the conurbation, here, too, both external and internal differentiation are
needed. The external definition is concerned largely with the
present green belt between towns and suburbs: how can it be
transformed into an actively landscaped, rather than neglected,
asset? The interior definition focuses on the housing itself, the
external face of private life, and the question of how to give it
communal force and meaning, whether through arrangement,
landscaping, or through public monuments, landmarks.

The response to this challenge takes a different form in areas
of growth and new development, and areas of regeneration and
renewal. In the areas of growth, the essential difficulty is the

inherently chaotic character of these new accretions of car-mobile clone homes, which have splintered urban identity into pre-packaged, defensive huddles. In that context, the architectural response has inevitably also been structured into small enclaves – enclaves of excellence and coherence, but enclaves all the same. Their very excellence only heightens the contrast with the grand collective civic spatial vision of nineteenth-century city develop-ment – which was also, of course, driven by private entrepreneurs! What should be the architectural response to this onslaught by the forces of 'family choice'? To begin with, any attempt to force 'tenements', 'public space' or 'urban mixed use' onto periphery dwellers is a futile exercise, in view of their undeniable preference for special segregated residential areas and for open-ended space and greenery, both private and public. This desire is one extreme within the range of opinions on the urban equation of freedom/individuality versus discipline/collectivity. Many of the people who go to live on the periphery are those who specially value openness and freedom. That even applied to some extent during the 1950s era of outer-suburban tenements. Recollections of the original inhabitants emphasise the impression of countryside greenness when they first moved in. And it certainly applies today. Some people go to live on the periphery for negative reasons, because of the lack of infrastructure within the cities, but many others do so simply because they like the life there. Our task is not in the least to deny that fact, but to exalt it spatially, as did the entrepreneurial suburb-builders of the nineteenth century. The choice is between passively accepting sprawl, and actively shaping new suburbs or suburban towns.

The core of this task is the regeneration of the vast, often depressed, schemes of public housing. Here, paradoxically, a prominent element of the existing stock is the twentieth-century equivalent of the tenements now so revered in the inner city. The main difference lies in their street plans, which are not grids but curvilinear layouts similar to the early New Towns: in fact, the architect who designed the tenements of Easterhouse, F. C. Scott, moved to East Kilbride New Town, where his almost identical

166

East Kilbride New Town

flats proved highly sought-after! As with the nineteenth-century inner clearance areas before them, the trajectory of these schemes' population has been sharply downwards, with consequent dereliction and loss of services. For example, Glasgow's Drumchapel has more than halved its population since 1971. For some architectural critics, both the problem and solution are simply stated: the Utopian cycle of rejection must continue. Glasgow writer Gavin Stamp, for example, points to the 'essential structural inadequacies of these estates – low density, incoherence, absence of true urban character, and . . . nothing of architectural merit'; their inhabitants are 'condemned to live without hope in a spiral of decline', and they should therefore be bulldozed back to 'parkland': 'wipe them out, and bring their long-suffering inhabitants back to the real city where they belong!'[40]

The people who live in those areas, of course, have different views about their identities and future. Just as in the old inner slum areas, the relative lack of mobility and the economic adversity has created an especially strong sense of local identity and territoriality, above all among children. In the view of their inhabitants, these outer areas should be revitalised, not liquidated. Over the past ten years, the concept of peripheral regeneration was also backed by the Tory government, despite its laissez-faire convictions. As part of the 1989 programme 'New Life for Urban Scotland', 'partnerships' of public authorities, private capital and community representatives were set up to regenerate four key deprived schemes: Whitfield in Dundee, Ferguslie Park in Paisley, Castlemilk in Glasgow and Wester Hailes in Edinburgh. More recently, the even more radical step has been proposed of wholesale transfer of problem areas to local regeneration companies.

But after nearly a decade, the material results in these and subsequent regeneration projects have been very uneven. The main impact has been in the built environment, especially in social housing. That amounts to rather a circular achievement, given that the environments being reconstructed were also, in their day, part of an attempt to revitalise the Scottish economy

Haddington

through social building. Overall, population loss has been accepted and institutionalised by large-scale house-rebuilding, reduction of density and tenure diversification. Economic and social improvements are unclear. In some areas, employment and household income stayed relatively stagnant. And all this vast building and investment activity leaves up in the air the central architectural and cultural issue of peripheral regeneration: that is, what kind of settlements or communities are these, or should they be? Are they autonomous villages, city-related suburbs, suburban towns – or something else?

In the next chapter, we will examine the potential of radical administrative changes as a way of addressing the peripheral scheme problems of Clydeside. Here, we are concerned with the spatial definition of Central Belt peripheral housing in general. This is a challenge not of shaping something new, but of reshaping something which already exists. Everybody accepts that these are areas, above all, of openness and freedom – but what form should that openness take? Should the aim of this grand programme of reordering and uplifting be to break down these areas completely into a fragmented agglomeration of enclaves, or should they be structured, albeit loosely, as city suburbs within an urban and regional framework, linked by better public transport, rather than unrestricted car use?

Until recently, the choice seems to have been overwhelmingly for the former, for an open embrace of market-driven anarchy. Across the regenerated schemes, the existing concrete tenements of mass-built socialist Clone City are being replaced by the mass-built two-storey brick boxes of laissez-faire Clone City, set in their introverted defensive-space clusters. In schemes such as Glasgow's Darnley, until only recently, there was (from today's perspective) a vast excess of indiscriminate open space and an almost crushing architectural homogeneity. Now, once everything has been chopped up and busied into countless 'domains', all that is left is enough space to form 'pocket parks' stocked with a few artworks. And the result is just as banal and repetitive as before!

170

Without in any way impeding the process of tenurial diversification and private involvement, those environmental problems could have been – and, in many cases, still could be – tackled directly through a more modest Eutopian strategy of layout and landscaping clarification, along with basic refurbishment and insulation, using as landmarks existing buildings such as the water towers which made possible these areas in the first place, or the tower blocks that still exist and mostly function well, despite the perverse Utopian dreams of people who want to tear them down. At the densities that are involved, we may find that the most important unifying element is not that of the buildings but of the open areas in between, and the key structuring role is that of the landscape architect. But there are also architectural ways in which we can build up collective or civic elements to help anchor the landscaped openness of the 'private' within new communities, through collective expression or degree of monumentality. In the traditional, focal city, it was above all the monuments of religious architecture and the public secular buildings such as schools and municipal centres that fulfilled that role in new suburbs. Even in the Modernist Age, the boldly assertive churches and public buildings constructed by architects such as Alan Reiach or Wheeler & Sproson in new towns and suburbs showed that it was possible to combine a rhetorical public face with monumental modern internal space. In 1959–64, for example, the building of a headquarters complex in Hamilton in the form of a lofty, elegant slab block, visible for miles around, allowed Lanark County Council to broadcast its aspirations to modernise a vast swathe of decayed industrial exurbia.

Now, however, this field of building has become diminished and fragmented. New churches are much more modest in size and few in numbers, while secular buildings of social character, such as medical centres and schools, are shrinking and assuming an insistently domestic face. At the same time, large buildings of a public-cum-commercial-consumption type are becoming ever bolder in design, as weapons in a war of towns and areas for competitive edge. By contrast, the self-contained complexes of modern industry, especially by inward investment companies, have, on the whole, maintained the order-giving Modernist and Beaux-Arts industrial-estate framework of low-density restraint, as islands of coherence in the exurban sprawl.

The building type which has raised in the most acute form these issues of secular monumentality on the periphery is one typical of today in its composite patronage patterns: the business or retail park, a postmodern variant of the industrial estate. The retail park, as a building type, is now in retreat, curbed by the rebalancing of land-use controls back towards city-centre retailing, along with tighter development design controls. But what it has done is to highlight the potential conflict of two Modernist demands: that for functional separation and parcellisation, and that for an order stemming from flowing continuous space. The result has been one of jarring incongruity, with vast acreages of haphazard car-parking and service areas, derived ultimately from Modernist flowing space, dotted anarchically with separate commercial gesture buildings and disconnected episodes of enclosure and formality.

How can any spatial integrity be achieved on the periphery, with its seemingly pervasive context of fragmentation? It may be that, in the long run, we can recover the aspiration to build collective complexes on a monumental scale. But more immediately and pragmatically, we can also aim at greater coherence in the way we arrange what we do build. One solution, learning from the influential mid-twentieth-century housing pattern of the Radburn system, separates sharply the public and private aspects of new developments by grouping buildings with service and vehicular functions on one side, and a civic landscaped environment on the other. This solution is attempted, with some success, in the Meier/Arnott layout of the Edinburgh Park development on the periphery of the capital, where all buildings face (without any direct access) the linear axis of what amounts to a major new public park, and service functions are gathered at the rear. Such a radical repudiation of today's mixed-use orthodoxies of promiscuous yet privatised use of space may meet with objections from

Sighthill housing project, Glasgow

the security-design experts, but do we really want a city designed by police officers? We can equally learn from the remodelling of public complexes of the Modernist postwar period, retaining their understated simplicity and room for the imagination, while reaching new balances of collective dignity and modern freedom, and incorporating the spatial links, flexibility of use and monumental highlights demanded today.

Lanark county headquarters, Hamilton

6
CITY PLACES – EAST AND WEST

NEW TOWNS: FROM IDEAL TO PLACE

How can these principles of Eutopian recovery be applied to the
actual cities and communities of Clydeforth? There can be no
better place to begin than with the new towns. Conceived as exem-
plars or prototypes, these have gradually naturalised themselves
as real places, bedding themselves into the existing local-authority
structure following the winding up of their governing Development
Corporations in 1996. The abolition of those authoritarian institutional foundations suggests that completely new settlements on
that scale are unlikely to be built again, especially as large-scale
greenfield development in general is increasingly problematic.
But the five new towns that already exist provide us with an
important bridge between the ideal and the specific.

The five new towns attempted a bold structuring of the drive
for freedom on the urban periphery, at a time of acute shortage
of land. And they have enjoyed a great deal of public popularity,
at the time and since. Between them, they present a wide variety
of solutions, of different densities and characters, which provide
Modern formulae of spatial ordering for all the different permutations of this 'dispersed edge' of open flux. By contrast, the
homogeneity of the engineer-designed municipal peripheral
schemes of the 1950s now seems to be so obsolete as to be incom-
prehensible. The main differentiating element of the five towns is
the varying extent to which they incorporate earlier embedded
communities. At one extreme, Cumbernauld, East Kilbride and
Livingston are essentially new conceptions, embracing some older
fragments. At the other extreme is the Mears formula of expanded
and regenerated new towns, based around several old nuclei, as
at Glenrothes and Irvine.

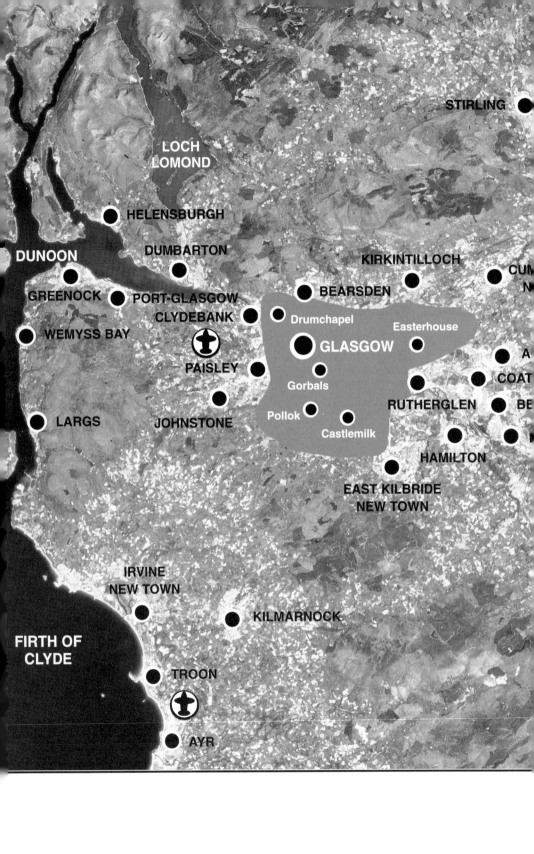

STIRLING

LOCH
LOMOND

HELENSBURGH

DUNOON

DUMBARTON

KIRKINTILLOCH

CUM
N

GREENOCK

PORT-GLASGOW

BEARSDEN

CLYDEBANK

Drumchapel

Easterhouse

A

WEMYSS BAY

GLASGOW

COAT

PAISLEY

Gorbals

RUTHERGLEN

BE

LARGS

JOHNSTONE

Pollok

Castlemilk

HAMILTON

EAST KILBRIDE
NEW TOWN

IRVINE
NEW TOWN

FIRTH OF
CLYDE

KILMARNOCK

TROON

AYR

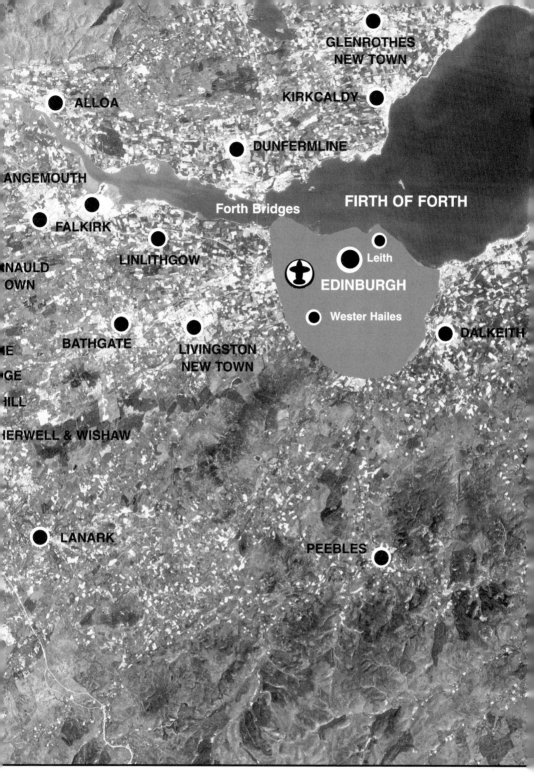

Clydeforth from space

Clone City

It is, perhaps, Cumbernauld which may be most directly relevant to the design of more highly structured suburbs or suburban towns for today. The urban design characteristics of its early phases sound like a shopping list of desiderata for the twenty-first-century urban periphery: compact planning and split-level flexibility, combined with private gardens for most households; spatial openness and views of the hills around, combined with enclosed domestic intimacy within the residential areas; sharp perimeter definition of the urban area to prevent piecemeal erosion of the countryside; and respect for the grey-green natural *genius loci* and immediacy of contact with nature, through a predominantly grey-and-white built image and flowing, forest-type landscaping. Expressed in the density figures beloved of the Modernist era, the early parts of Cumbernauld are around 95 ppa, compared with 120 ppa in the later, slightly harder and more urban areas of the town. To put those figures into context, roughly similar densities to Cumbernauld, of around 100 ppa, are found in the dispersed tenemental plans of both the 1950s peripheral schemes and today's 'new' Gorbals, whereas densities were rather higher in the 1960s tower block redevelopment of the Gorbals (165 ppa) and 'successful' middle-class pre-1914 areas of four-storey tenements in Edinburgh and Glasgow (around 200 ppa).

While Cumbernauld seems the most relevant inspiration for areas of intensity on the periphery, or for new suburban towns, more loosely structured suburbs can equally draw on the precedent of the earlier, lower-density neighbourhoods of East Kilbride New Town (around 60–70 ppa) – mainly composed of two-storey cottages and three-storey flats in profuse but more 'domestic' greenery, interspersed with isolated tower blocks for higher-income small households. The density of East Kilbride, around 60–70 ppa, is similar to that of some of the most architecturally ordered peripheral developments of recent years, such as E & F McLachlan's infill project of 1996 at the Gyle, Edinburgh (65 ppa). A similar pattern applies in the case of the excellent planned settlements, short of full new town status, that were built by the Scottish Special Housing Association mainly in the 1970s: for example,

Erskine, a mini-new town developed with Renfrew County Council in 1972–83.

For reconstruction strategies combining elements of periphery along with existing town nuclei, the most recently built of the new towns, Irvine, is of particular relevance because of its highly differentiated combination of focal and open planning. Irvine took up the Glenrothes and Mears theme of nucleated intensification of existing decayed industrial towns, through a twin-track strategy. This combined the mainstream Modernist means of large-scale new construction and zoned land use, alongside a conservative surgery regeneration of existing burghs and villages embedded within the pattern. An original 1960s target population of 116,000 was eventually scaled down by around half. What has resulted is a unique experiment, a combination of Geddesian place and rooted order with the spatial freedom and open functional differentiation inherited from Modernist and earlier Scottish urbanism. In a clear challenge to today's panacea of mixed-use urban villages and 'density' for everyone and every place, the entire area of Irvine is subdivided into distinctively zoned areas: 'historic burgh' centres with small-scale special-needs new infills; a megastructure-like town-centre commercial complex; separate residential and industrial districts of a crafts-like elegance; and parkland and leisure areas. There is even a specialist heritage theme-park zone, intended to channel and control in one place the impulse of the present day towards the popular, commercialised exploitation of heritage, and including an area of Mackintosh-influenced modern flats.

The planning and development of Irvine as a whole was made possible partly by the dirigiste New Town tradition, now of course defunct, but also partly by the pride of the old small-burgh civic tradition: the first steps in the plan were taken by Irvine Town Council in 1959; so the project always had one foot in the existing civic and local world. After the abolition of the Development Corporation in 1996, the vision of its architects and planners, including George Wren and chief designer Roan Rutherford, has begun to take a more place-specific slant. Wren and Rutherford

Irvine New Town

Cumbernauld New Town

Paisley town centre

Cumbernauld, Seafar housing area

have together set up a new private practice, which has begun to
establish the outlines of a regional Modernism for the south-west.
The legacy of Irvine is a Scottish Modernist vision of place combined with space, a vision of modern freedom rooted in the centuries-old tradition of urban order and planned settlement, at
both the small-town and the city scale. It provides a powerful
alternative voice which can inform our own efforts of the future
at the reshaping of our 'old' towns and, even, city regions.

The absorption of the new towns into their hinterlands has
negative as well as positive aspects. Freed from the close designer
control of the Development Corporations, they, too, are now being
swamped by a sea of brick clone homes around their carefully
defined urban peripheries. And some of them are experiencing
the same social problems as the older urban centres. As a result,
their own growth is now also in need of rectification and clarification. They, too, have become invaded by Clone City. That does
not prevent us, however, from learning from them valuable lessons
in urban and peripheral differentiation. This time, we should try
to do even better. If a shift in emphasis to public transport, and
thus a cut in the inflexibility of road and parking provision, can
be realised on a large scale on the periphery, then even greater
variety in planning can be achieved than in the New Towns, free
of the social problems consequent on the postwar pressure for
output and speed.

OLD TOWNS IN NEW SPACES:
RE-IMAGINING THE FORTH VALLEY

We have argued that Clydeforth must be conceived as a single,
linear city constellation, with a consolidation and cross-fertilisation
of the existing focal and open frameworks, and of their respective
concerns with old town and modern city. The aim must be to open
out the east, without anarchy, and to re-embed the west, without
fundamentalism. Both the freedom and generosity of space of
Modernist regional planning, and the order and *genius loci* differentiation of urban settlement in its landscape roots can be

applied not just in west and east respectively, but freely across the conurbation as required. The Modernist zoning concept can be expanded to encompass the specialisation of whole cities rather than just districts, contrasting east and west without any longer destructively polarising them. The Clydeforth strategy is one of unity in diversity, a diversity in which a reinvigorated east-west contrast plays the central role.

Of the two, it is the east, not the west, which now superficially appears to be in the greater crisis. This is a crisis of congestion, but one caused by prosperity rather than by slum conditions. In Edinburgh, mounting economic and political pressures threaten to overwhelm the city's careful processes of cumulative development and the sedimentation of visions which has resulted from them. Over the past two centuries, a constant balancing of old and new, and an orderly, radial pattern of city extension, made it possible to avoid grand, all-embracing crises of self-regeneration. That balance still generally applies, and has even become further entrenched with the growing power of the city's conservationists from the 1970s. In particular, owing to the avoidance of mass clearances of the nineteenth-century fabric, there is no sharp break in the substance of the city, equivalent to that around the centre of Glasgow: only in the harbour areas of Leith and Granton is there a substantial zone of brownfield land. But the new pressures of development are beginning to break apart these careful relationships, through a combination of massive image buildings in central gap sites – including the Lothian Road commercial zone master-planned by Terry Farrell, and the tent-like visitor centre designed by Michael Hopkins for the site opposite the Holyrood parliament – with Clone City sprawl along the periphery and harbour-side. There is a growing discrepancy between the fierce conservation protection of the city's established heritage as a spatial expression of collective and civic vision, and the extreme individualism of this new commercial and residential work. Between these extremes, with their intense demand and rising property values, the city's low-income groups are being gradually squeezed into less and less desirable interstices.

187

Street crossing, Edinburgh New Town

River crossing, Kincardine-on-Forth

Clone City

Yet the crisis is not as serious as it might seem, given that its cause is prosperity, not poverty. There is at least the possibility of adequately resourced remedies. And a ready-made solution is to hand: the formula of urban containment and population over-spill already devised fifty years ago by Abercrombie and Matthew for Glasgow and Clydeside, adjusted to take account of the Edinburgh and east-coast traditions of focal planning. On the one hand, the 'old town', now redefined as the entire existing city, can be entrenched behind its sharp borders of water to the north and the outer ring road to the south, borders which are accentuated by a new and harder architectural edge overlooking a more proactively regulated green belt. On the other hand, population and employment can be overspilled beyond the green belt to a 'constellation' of expanded towns (in Mears's expression), linked to the capital by radically upgraded public transport.

In the city's centre and the inner areas, the crushing intensity of the conservation blanket has to be offset not so much by large clearances and gesture buildings, as by conservative surgery interventions. But the essence of Geddes's original conservative surgery projects in the Old Town was to create small glimpses of openness and green space in the urban core – in other words, to open up and slightly dislocate the 'continuous fabric'. Today, that approach is impeded in its use of the small sites available, by a combination of the assumption of enclosed tenemental form and the effect of motor-age bureaucracy, especially the stipulations of residents' car-parking and road widths, in sterilising much ground space. This rigidity is now being challenged in a number of projects, including a pioneering car-free housing infill on a small brownfield site in the industrial suburb of Gorgie, and John Hope's 1992 masterplan for the Holyrood regeneration area, on the edge of the Old Town, which attempts to reconcile a respect for the area's medieval layout with glimpses of space and openness through the use of denser and higher blocks. Some Edinburgh architects working in that area or more generally in the inner city, such as Richard Murphy, Arcade, Malcolm Fraser and Ungless & Latimer, set out to create modern freedom through an organic approach which contrasts the heavy, masonry deposits of the Old Town with lighter interventions or insertions in that fabric. Others, such as Neil Gillespie of Reiach & Hall, take the classical New Town as their starting point, and try to introduce more neutral or muted modernist spaces in reflection of enlightenment and east-coast severity.[41]

Around the edge of the city, there is a more ambitious task of establishing order in the face of spreading market chaos, fixing a hard edge to juxtapose with the landscape. On the city's sharp landward edge to the south-west, where a strong landscape definition is provided by the nearness of the Pentland Hills, the task is not to do away with the frayed green belt, but to reinforce it with a more emphatic urban border to the ring road, possibly including new landmark buildings. This firm cordon can be offset by opening out along the entire frontage to the Forth. In Leith, the task is less that of healing a clearance-ravaged area, as on many parts of the Clyde, as of integrating the city with an incomparable water view and clearing away the clutter of light industry and retail parks that has accumulated along the waterfront.

In view of the city's shortage of brownfield sites, it is beyond the current built-up limits that the main issues of land pressure will be decided. Here, at the moment, the only formula on offer is that of the further spread of Clone City. It is vital that the South-East Wedge proposal, promoted as a dense urban village interspersed with belts of greenery, should not in reality turn out to be an amorphous blot. Aided by fast rail services and the restraining of private-car access to the city, the search for housing sites, and potentially even office and other employment sites, must move decisively beyond the city boundaries, to places such as the former Midlothian, East Lothian and southern Fife coalfield communities, and the West Lothian shale mining areas. This must be done not by resuscitating the grandiose new town development techniques of the Modernist age, but by building on existing communities, including the small historic burghs on both banks of the Forth, and the former industrial burghs concentrated

Edinburgh Royal Infirmary

Grangemouth Refinery

in clusters in the Lothians, southern Fife and Stirlingshire. In these, the existing challenge is not so much one of restraining growth or of coping with the aftermath of mass redevelopment, as one of a gradual, piecemeal economic and social expansion or regeneration.

Up until now, the knitting together of old mining communities in the east by new towns has been attempted only on a relatively large scale, at Glenrothes in Fife and Livingston in West Lothian. Both of these combine a generally low-density urbanism with infiltration by fingers of countryside, but do so on a scale that would be environmentally unacceptable nowadays. It is the Mears formula of much smaller and more flexible new towns, of around 10,000–15,000 population, and attached to existing communities under regeneration, which is far more suited to our needs today. And the postwar school of Geddesian modernism along the east coast by architects such as Wheeler & Sproson or Baxter, Clark & Paul did much to give an architectural shape to these ideas, by reinvigorating existing smaller historic nuclei through sensitive social housing redevelopments: planner Frank Tindall's 1960s extensions to historic Haddington, to accommodate Glasgow overspill, also provide a notable precedent. In any move to revitalise the Forth Valley along constellation lines, these ideas will become highly relevant once again – as will the experience at Irvine in the west, in the incorporation of several historic centres within a Modernist extension plan. The Irvine formula of variegated focal points within a zoned framework is well suited to some of the Forth Valley's urban groupings: for instance, that of Falkirk and Grangemouth, with its combination of historic industrial burgh with low-density housing and modern industry on a heroic scale.

BLACK HOLES AND BORDERS:
THE RESURRECTION OF THE CLYDE VALLEY

The crisis of Glasgow and the west is of a more insidious, yet more pervasive kind than that of the capital. The reconstruction strategy of the century from the 1870s to the 1970s succeeded all too well in its double aim: to provide Clydesiders with modern homes, and to remove completely the industrial congestion of Glasgow. A new and dispersed network of communities was created, but, in that era of mass warfare, one could not expect this to be done by consensus. Instead, there were the two violently conflicting approaches of the Clyde Valley Plan, with its radical dispersal and overspill, and of Glasgow Corporation's Bruce Plan, with its proposal to contain the whole process within the city's boundaries. The bitter conflict between the two strategies, over three decades from the 1940s to the 1970s, has left an enduring spatial and social legacy in the form of sharp polarisations and gaps. This especially applies in the inner areas of Glasgow, where the housing-planning clashes left huge swathes of cleared but unused land, and on the periphery of Glasgow, where the tenemental schemes built by the city in the 1950s, in a desperate attempt to resist overspill pressures by site cramming, glower across the green belt at the overspill 'reception towns' and new towns beyond.

Despite over thirty years of attempts to heal these scars, first through strategic planning initiatives by Strathclyde Region, and now through a host of 'market' and 'enterprise' initiatives, the problem today seems, if anything, further from solution than ever. For example, hundreds of millions of pounds have been spent in the attempts to regenerate the Castlemilk scheme alone, but large swathes of it are still semi-derelict. This is, in contrast to the prosperity crisis of the capital, a genuinely serious and structural problem, a problem which cannot be papered over by Glasgow's continuing success in attracting cultural festivals and awards. The city, with its shrinking population and resources, especially after it had to sell off its assets to maintain services in the 1980s, now simply does not have the means to tackle these vast areas of dereliction and dilapidated social infrastructure, especially in view of the skyrocketing costs of brownfield land decontamination. Yet it has to continue, as much as ever, to play host to the leisure, cultural and commercial needs of all the surrounding towns and suburbs. These social-economic problems

North Edinburgh

South Glasgow

constitute a black hole at the centre of the nation's largest population grouping, a hole which, if not filled, will eventually begin to undermine the country's overall economic and social integrity. Clearly, to do nothing is not an option.

Following the end of state-socialist planning, with its advocacy of overarching intervention, this challenge of renewal now falls within the responsibility of the new capitalist agencies of urban regeneration. Some of the emerging strategies are logical and, probably, inescapable responses to the need to attract private capital: for example, the proposal to transfer Glasgow City Council's entire housing stock to community bodies. In the field of planning, however, the impact of the new market-driven framework has so far been less positive. The signs are increasingly pointing to a rejection of the Clyde Valley Plan dispersal framework and a resuscitation of the Bruce Plan, now as an umbrella for the market anarchy of Clone City. We noted the generic, nationwide themes of current urban regeneration policies earlier in this chapter. But for the black hole of Clydeside, a specific and specially strong version is in the process of being concocted. From architectural and planning commentators, on the one hand, we have fundamentalist rhetoric to legitimise the project, which no one expects to see literally implemented. It argues that the peripheral housing schemes should be liquidated and their inhabitants 'returned' to the city, which will be 'restored' to its old, tenemental integrity. From the economic development consultants comes a more pragmatic, practical programme which could actually be implemented. What both have in common is a determination that Glasgow's problems should be solved within its boundaries, to underline its status as 'a great European city'. Development rights to the green belt can be sold to Clone City house-builders, to develop right up to the city boundaries with brick boxes. The profits from this could be used to subsidise 'planning gain' redevelopment of the peripheral tenement schemes, again with little brick boxes, and to pay for brownfield decontamination in inner Glasgow, allowing its regeneration with neo-tenemental urban villages, and new roads to tie together the myriad private enclaves.

This strategy, driven by honest necessity and by the best of intentions, nevertheless differs from the 1945–6 Bruce Plan in one vital respect: in its lack of an overarching spatial order and integrity. The Bruce Plan's self-contained solution was one of vast Beaux-Arts dignity and hierarchy, with office skyscrapers in the centre, tenement-lined boulevards in the inner suburbs and spacious garden cities on the periphery; and the plan fell apart largely because of the huge cost of that grandiosity. The result of the present strategy would certainly be to fill in the black hole – but with the anarchic, car-fuelled sprawl of Clone City. And its example of fragmentation and polarisation would spread out across Clydeside: already, other, wealthier suburbs outside the city, such as Bearsden and Milngavie, are pursuing their own, separate agendas of land extension for speculative building, leaving poorer towns languishing with their own intractable problems. That could, of course, be tackled in turn by extending Glasgow's boundaries again so as to gobble up these richer suburban areas, but to do so would only displace and compound the problem. The Clyde Valley Plan showed that Clydeside must be viewed as a whole, and any attempt to turn back the clock towards self-containment or 'imperial Glasgow', however much encouraged by today's oppositional local-government system or dressed up in the new language of European city rivalry, cannot endure in the long run.

We cannot walk away from the openness and dispersal achieved by the century of reconstruction. But that structure must be given greater coherence and economic viability. It is the concept of Clydeforth which, for the first time, allows us to do this, by grafting the focal city-planning concepts of the east onto the decentralised Clydeside urban system. Glasgow and the west cannot achieve this on its own. Not even Strathclyde Region would have had sufficient power to do so. This is a national problem, and its resolution is a strategic organisational and infrastructural task for the new Scottish government. Transport is a key ingredient. As we noted above, improved west-east rail links will play a central role in stemming any eastwards population flow. Within Clydeside, the need is for a Eutopian strategy, building on the urban structure we have inherited, rather than discarding it. It would be intolerably wasteful and destructive to wipe out the Glasgow peripheral schemes or submerge the entire city in clone boxes. But their problems cannot be solved within their present relationship to the city.

Our view is that the institutional, municipal boundaries of Clydeside have now become a serious obstacle to creative and dynamic solutions, and should be radically redrawn and reinterpreted so as to redistribute both the problems and the opportunities of the region. The aim should be to create an array of new 'border cities' around Glasgow, each centred on a focal large town, but also taking in nearby wealthier suburbia (hitherto outside Glasgow) and depressed Glasgow peripheral schemes. Glasgow itself can then concentrate on tackling its inner dereliction problems through more innovative and dense patterns. In other words, we carry the Clyde Valley Plan formula to its conclusion, creating a completely open framework stretching down the Clyde Valley, but we anchor this framework in focal communities. In place of the old oppositional formula of Glasgow versus the green belt and the rest, now the entire urban zone is treated as a single landscape unit, its internal spaces closely controlled, and sharply defined on the exterior by the new, displaced outer green border of hills and water.

What would be the implications for the city of Glasgow itself of such a consummation of the Clyde Valley Plan? Clearly, within the city, the germs exist for a focal system of planning. Glasgow, compared to a doughnut in the 1970s and 1980s, at the height of the demolitions, is now more like an irregularly woven tapestry studded with gaps. These gaps are a mixture of embedded 'old towns' of nineteenth-century or earlier date, interwoven with Modernist redevelopments or new developments that now themselves require regeneration.

The biggest of these 'old towns' is the city centre, since the 1970s defined forcefully on three sides by the inner ring road motorway and the river. The inner ring road, a linear park which brought such a decisive element of modern openness to inner Glasgow, has paradoxically ruptured the old open continuity around the centre, and has encouraged the development of heritage enclave tendencies previously identified with Edinburgh and the east. The city's days of bulldozing monumentality are over. Central Glasgow, as much as Edinburgh, now sees itself as a Geddesian narrative city. But, in a continuation of the old openness, this tendency has taken root in patches, in a polycentric form rather than in the integrated connections of Edinburgh, in discrete areas such as the Merchant City, Cathedral, West End, Garnethill. This greater room to breathe, by comparison with Edinburgh, means that there is no suffocating opposition of conservation and modernity. Instead, there is a hybrid of modernity and heritage focused on the cult of Mackintosh, which provides a familiar backdrop to help make sense of changing ideological positions about modernity and the city. It links intellectual concepts of the city with capitalist marketing and the Postmodern cult of the individual hero architect.

Beyond the centre's boundaries, the old scarred landscape of mass clearance has been infilled into a much more complex pattern. Strands of relatively well embedded building stretch out along the original main radial roads, comprising a mixture of restored nineteenth-century tenements, the remains of surviving nineteenth-century industrial heritage, and 1980s neo-tenement infill built on formerly cleared land, like the 'Maryhill Corridor'. These are separated by the remnants of the clearances and large dilapidated areas of twentieth-century housing, including tenements and tower blocks. Five per cent of the total area of the city was completely derelict in 1990. The effect of the current regeneration strategy for this vast zone, driven very largely by the spiralling costs of brownfield land decontamination, is to polarise future development between money-making Clone City sprawl, stretching inwards from the city boundaries as far towards the

Central Greenock

Outer Motherwell

centre as can be economically sustained, and 'traditional tene-mental' low-rise flats on the inner brownfield sites: in other words, fundamentalism and consumerist anarchy feeding off one another.

Under the strategy just set out, this mutually destructive rela-tionship would not be possible: the city boundary would no longer include the large outer schemes. New and more flexible ways need to be devised to intensify development on inner land, and at the same time to create a greater sense of urban identity, needs which are denied by the homogeneity and lack of civic scale of today's mixed-use tenement formula. Could a return to the selective building of high blocks in landmark locations – now, emphatically, only for those who choose to live in them – especially in car-free projects near railway stations and other public-trans-port centres, help begin to fill in the black hole without colossal land reclamation costs?

The problematic aspects of the attempts to reconstruct 'tradi-tional' inner Glasgow are encapsulated in the projects and debates surrounding one inner area in particular: the renowned Gorbals. In a century and a half, this district has undergone three succes-sive dramatic processes of development, culminating in today's demolitions of Modernist deck blocks and towers designed by Sir Basil Spence. Although situated immediately adjacent to the city centre, at the moment the Gorbals is largely made up of undiffer-entiated open space, roads and scraps of Modernist developments. The first major re-redevelopment section, the Crown Street ini-tiative (from 1992), was founded on a trenchant rejection of the spatial and social concepts of Modernism. It was initially con-ceived as a mixed-use revival of the 'traditional' Glasgow tenement street, with its demarcated public and private zones. But later phases have become increasingly sympathetic to Modernism once more. In the nearby Gorbals East area, the centrepiece is a new oval-plan villa block by Elder & Cannon, whose forceful form engages in a dialogue with neighbours and sets out to provide a new landmark centrepiece for the ravaged area. But even here, thorny questions remain, in relation to the centuries-old Scottish drive to order the city through openness and space. In the context of the Gorbals as it has developed over 150 years, is it feasible to throw this process into reverse, to recreate an old-style dense community spirit? And how can we create new landmarks using blocks which are dwarfed by the high tower blocks all around? Which is more respectful of the spirit of place: to mentally edit out these huge objects, or to restructure the area carefully around them?

Now that the hectoring monumentality of Spence's slab blocks no longer overshadows the area, the quiet sobriety of Robert Matthew's neighbouring section of the Gorbals, north of Ballater Street (1958–64), can be better appreciated – despite the silly Postmodernist roofs added to its four towers. Here, we are in no doubt that we are in a city, yet we have space to be ourselves. We enjoy the truly individual privacy which is guaranteed by Modern anonymity, at the same time as a calm sense of the collective – unlike the frenetically designed quality of today's village home enclaves. And in other areas where urban design and landscaping of this sort were attempted on a larger scale, such as the Scottish Special Housing Association's Wyndford project in Maryhill (1961–9), there are even better examples of what might be achieved by a combination of urban enclosure and Modern freedom.

Thus, in contrast to the originally highly polemical anti-Modernist formulation of the Crown Street Gorbals project, might it not be worth concentrating on intensifying and clarifying what we already have, building up carefully around the towers with complementary, lower-height interventions – and then extending the same general formula to other inner areas in need of the rebuilding of structure and identity? The possibility of revisiting the issues of experimentation in dense house types for new patterns of inner-city living is raised by the Homes for the Future demonstration project, located on a group of infill sites in an industrial inner suburb overlooking Glasgow Green. Its elements include apartment blocks by Elder & Cannon, Ian Ritchie and Rick Mather, a stepped block with cascading terraces by Eisaku

Port Glasgow town centre

The Gorbals and Glasgow city centre

Ushida & Kathryn Findlay, and a hybrid row house/apartment group by McKeown Alexander. RMJM, the firm descended ultimately from Robert Matthew's practice, has contributed a four-storey block of flats with a linked tower of maisonettes. And the row-house tradition of small private gardens is given a novel twist of Modernist open planning in Wren Rutherford's four-storey mini-tower block for Mactaggart & Mickel, with its ground-floor wheelchair flat and upper-floor workspace-maisonette, both with patio and conservatory. Could this project be a stepping stone to a wider plan for the revitalisation of the areas surrounding the Green, and on across the inner districts of Glasgow?

BORDER-CITIES

Just as Glasgow's new 'inner centres' can draw on both focal and open planning, so too could the new or consolidated places of the periphery. Here the formula of the new towns is once again highly relevant, through the way in which natural landscape has been actively exploited there to create real places out of left-over green belt, and in which, especially at Irvine, old towns have been used to anchor a wide scatter of new areas. Our aim must be not to abandon, but to complete the Abercrombie–Matthew framework of dispersal, by throwing down the mid-century barriers of confrontation, and heightening still further the urban-rural contrast.

The 1996 abolition of the special status of the new towns has begun the process of anchoring them in their localities, and bridging the damaging split within social urbanism between them and the shoddily built Glasgow peripheral schemes. Arguably, it was the state-directed building of the new towns themselves, with their preferential treatment and subsidies, and their exclusion of unskilled workers and old urban problems, which extended the centuries-old processes of class residential segregation on Clydeside into a region-wide social schism. Now that is already beginning to be healed, for instance by encouraging a mobility of labour from Glasgow's Castlemilk to the East Kilbride electronics industry, and radically reducing long-term unemployment in Castlemilk. We now need to go a stage further, by throwing down the administrative boundaries that separate them.

By ceasing to treat both the new towns and peripheral schemes as places apart, and integrating them with the older Clydeside communities, we can define the outer edge of Clydeside with a ring of new border-cities – highly differentiated urban clusters separated by actively designed landscaping, but freed from destructive competition with one another. The old industrial towns around Glasgow are ready now to assume their focal role, having discarded their old ideas of shame or materialistic negligence and instead taken aim at new aspirations of cultural identity – as demonstrated, for example, in Merrylees Grierson & Robertson's new Motherwell Heritage Centre (1996), a project directly inspired by the Geddesian philosophy of place, work and folk, and intended to open the eyes of the Motherwell community to the richness of their legacy, good and bad.[42] But the transformation is not yet complete: less than two miles away from the Motherwell centre lies the huge site of the demolished Ravenscraig steelworks, a vast regeneration opportunity which, it has to be hoped, will not be squandered and fragmented.

In contrast to the Forth, with its widely separated north- and south-bank communities, the Clyde plays a significant role in the internal ordering of its region. Even today, in an era of scaled-down planning aspirations, it is a platitude that the Clyde provides the main challenge and opportunity for a strategic vision within the region. But its unifying role has changed radically, from an industrial and communications artery to a more metaphoric, symbolic one. The river has become the potential trigger for a cycle of regeneration of regional identity: a kind of linear park, like the motorways before it, but without the utilitarian associations of mass car transport. The challenges of regeneration along the Clyde are now more complex than simply converting old docks and grain silos into cultural centres and offices. Its configuration affects the way in which we imagine, or reimagine, the urban relationships of the region to form new clusters or border-cities. In

general, within the older industrial areas, there has been a
change from the assumption of a relatively closed, self-contained
river to an openness and permeability; and the point at which,
despite that openness, the river still becomes a significant barrier
to communication, is a key psychic dividing line. To the east of
that line is a ring of communities with the city at the centre. To its
west is an estuarine grouping, at present largely divided into two,
but potentially unifiable by bridge links.

In some cases, the present-day old or new towns immediately
ringing Glasgow, with their sharp sense of local cultural-spatial
identity, provide highly suitable foci for the creation of border-
cities: for example, Paisley, Renfrew and Barrhead in combination
with the Pollok district of outer Glasgow; or Clydebank, Bearsden
and Milngavie in combination with Glasgow's Drumchapel. In
others, the situation is more like that of some of the post-1945
new towns, as the existing communities are smaller and a more
active development policy is needed to knit them together: for
instance, the area to the north-east of Glasgow, with its scatter of
small burghs (for example, Kirkintilloch), Glasgow peripheral
schemes (for example, Easterhouse) and old mining villages (for
example, Gartcosh). Further to the west, the problems are
polarised more sharply between the legacies of obsolete heavy
industry in some places, and the relics of lowest-common-denom-
inator leisure provision in others. Both aspects are forced together,
in microcosm, in the Inverclyde group of towns (Greenock,
Gourock, Port Glasgow) on the south bank of the Clyde, a place
of an almost incredible potential sense of identity, but at present
of very little realised urban achievement. Here, in a place where
the outer landscape border of Clydeforth is pinched in almost to
the very edge of the Clyde, we find an incomparable topographic
location, terraced on precipitous slopes down to the river; a
highly distinctive linear functional differentiation of industrial
'east end' and residential, seaside 'west end'; a superb municipal
headquarters zone; and even a special local variety of tenement,
with high plinth, tailor made to the steep slopes. The contribution
of the twentieth century to this has consisted of a few notable

churches and public buildings, but otherwise numbers of housing schemes and tower blocks that take very little advantage of the magnificent site. And the area has appalling social problems, ranging from mass housing dampness to an especially chaotic example of bus deregulation, which in their own right demand radical intervention in its infrastructure.

Elsewhere in the estuary, on both sides of the river, on peninsulas and islands, the predominant challenge is that of a stagnating social-economic structure combining a low-quality leisure industry and dependence on declining military activity. All along the river, there are unexpected pockets of decay. For example: what hope can there be for the revitalisation of the Clyde as an artery of recreation and tourism when the jewel of the estuary, the town of Rothesay in its majestic bay, presents to the disembarking visitor a face dominated by collapsed, subsiding and derelict buildings, interspersed with squalid snack bars and new single-storey infill structures? Even the most outwardly prosperous Clyde towns stand on shifting foundations – in the case of Helensburgh, literally so, in view of the removable structures of the nearby submarine base on which its economy depends! Inland, are pockets of decay more closely related to the patterns of Central Clydeside, especially in the former mining villages of Ayrshire.

At the mouth of the Clyde, 'place, work and folk' is not so much an abstract slogan as a call to action, a summons to bring together a magnificent site and urgent need, and to synthesise them with grandeur, whether by traditional means or by Modernist spatial principles, to make a true 'border-city'.

The only real remedy lies, again, in the long term, in a strategic policy of integrated economic-social regeneration, including a restructuring of the tourist industry away from the cheap and nasty. But the framing of such a strategy would be a complex task. Certainly, new road or rail bridge links across the estuary – for example, between Gourock and Dunoon, or Port Glasgow and Cardross – could knit together its disparate communities, open up a psychic window to Argyll and the Highlands, and reduce the umbilical Glasgow dependency complex. But these would have to

Dunoon

Clydebank

be accompanied by strict safeguards against encouragement of
the nomadic car-mobility of Clone City, whether by commuters or
tourists. Only within the wider context of a reimagined Clydeforth, closely tied by rapid public transport not only to Glasgow
but to the pressure-cooker capital, could the Clyde estuary begin
a real and enduring revival.

Monument to reconciliation: the meeting of Pope and
Moderator at New College, 1982

7
CONCLUSION
Monuments to the Future

The Scottish city has played a complex role in definitions of the nation's collective identity, because of its enduring material presence within society. It has absorbed and refracted its cultural context and its natural, topographical setting. It has made an abstract, monumental poetry out of them. And that monumentality, in turn, itself has provided an exemplary narrative, the narrative of heritage, to help reinforce and reshape society's wider perception of itself. Under the old, integrated unionist identities of Scotland – as the nation of enterprising Improvement, triumphal imperialism or social welfarism – architecture benefited powerfully from their vigour and idealism. And its own autonomous monumentality helped regulate change and re-embed those identities. What, then, are the implications for Scottish architecture of the sea change in identity that was signalled on the home-rule referendum day, 11 September 1997?

To begin with, it is a paradox that the new Scottish government is being set up at a time of a global trend towards 'less government', and a decline in legitimacy of both old-style authoritarian nationalism and materialist ideas of progress. In the 1970s, arguments about home rule focused on economic interests and the oil question. The aspiration was for a state-led social policy involving massive public expenditure. But since then, in the words of social policy academic Richard Parry, the home-rule cause has become 'less a search for policy development than an expression of political identity . . . an assertion of the democratic right of the Scottish people.'[43] As a result, many of the hopes being expressed in anticipation of home-rule democracy have the ring of platitudes or tautologies: that it will be modern, consensual, egalitarian, driven by intellectual idealism, or even just that it will be defined by a special sense of community – a claim which, of course, is common to absolutely all national identities or nationalisms everywhere.

The same has applied, so far, to discussions of home rule's relationship to architecture. As we noted above, those debates have focused solely on the representational or symbolic role of the new parliament building, to which the same broad expectations have simply been transferred: that it will be open to the people, planned so as to discourage confrontation, equipped with the latest computer technology, and so forth. But, quite apart from the fact that such generalised qualities are not specific to any country – indeed, the Austrian turn-of-century architect Otto Wagner claimed that democracy was a universal attribute of all modern Western culture – these claims are also undermined by their assumption of a simple correspondence of political aspiration and architectural representation. That was something that might have seemed plausible earlier this century, despite the constant shifting of styles and their associations during the Historicist Age. But it certainly cannot satisfy us now, in this era of fundamental questioning of the unity of signifier and signified. Under Post-modernism, 'architecture as representation' can all too easily become 'architecture as image-making'. In such circumstances, the difference between a symbolic national institution and a theme-park pavilion could shrink almost to vanishing point, and the gulf between image and reality could become unbridgeable. After all, as one Scottish political party leader neatly put it, 'a real Scottish Parliament would be impressive meeting in a tent in the Meadows'.[44]

In fact, the most potent life forces in Scottish society today are expressions not of strength, unification and assertion – the typical components of the old, aggressive nationalisms of the nineteenth and early twentieth centuries – but of the abnegation of those urges. We cannot confidently say where we are going, but we know what we have left behind. Our new freedoms are defined by the repudiation not just of bombastic imperialism, but also of all the other, subtler assertions of the old Scottish solidarities, such as militant Presbyterianism, 'Red Clydeside', and even the 'democratic intellect' tradition. The dissolution of these identities is traceable throughout the built environment, where the old structures of domination defined by municipal boundaries, church steeples and council housing stocks are, today, in collapse. The built form in which that collapse has, up to now, expressed itself is the anarchy of Clone City; yet if we can take collective control of Clone City, this dissolution can equally become a great liberation.

To encapsulate these elusive processes of renewal in any single new building is almost impossible. That fact is poignantly under-lined by the effortless symbolic power of the old building chosen to house the temporary, inaugural home-rule parliament: the Church of Scotland General Assembly Hall and New College complex on The Mound in Edinburgh. New College is such a wonderful architectural symbol of our emancipation from old divisions, not so much because of its exhilarating architecture, masterfully crafted by Playfair and Bryce, but because of its history – because of what it once was, but is no longer. Seventy years ago, it would have been unthinkable that this building, the proud emblem of militant Protestantism, with all its domineering divisiveness, could ever serve as a symbol of national unity. Now, seventeen years after the meeting of Pope John Paul II with the Moderator of the Kirk beneath John Knox's statue, the unthinkable has actually happened!

In contrast to the ceaseless debates about the form and sym-bolism of the new parliament building, we have sketched out in this book a radically different vision of how architecture can help build a new Scottish identity. Our vision is not confined to the imagery of elite national institutions, but addresses the environ-ment we all inhabit. It does so not through pious aspirations, but through calls for practical acts, such as the development of new planning frameworks; the regeneration and reunification of Clydeforth; and the use of environmental education to remedy the alienation of many people from the places they inhabit, and the injustice and exclusion which results. Inevitably, in a short book such as this, we have only been able to sketch out these aims in initial outline, rather than in detail.

Clone City

The boundaries and certainties of the old Scotland, whether spatial or social, are inexorably dissolving. What is to replace them? Our argument is that, by harnessing and transforming today's rampant 'clone' of the conurbation, by drawing new boundaries of civic and national life, we can contribute to a real empowerment, rather than merely an empty image of empowerment. Through taking up and developing the Neotechnic vision of Geddes and others, the possibility opens up of a real democracy of city-building, bound together by mutual responsibilities and commitments, not least the duty to ensure that the future we plan lives up to the legacy of our past. Within that new democracy, one of the most important participants will be that of the home-rule government itself, in its role as ringmaster and regulator. Because this synthesis is founded on place along with folk, it can also become a real, rather than just rhetorical, unifying force; by helping overcome the real divisions within the country, and within individual towns and cities, it can help prevent Scottish democracy from being diverted into a typical global-marketplace battle between competing cities and interest groups. And because the issues which it tackles are issues of globalisation, issues which trouble people all over the world, the challenge of Clone City can engage this country with international debates at a level of common reality – in contrast to the vacuous marketing hype of the cult of C. R. Mackintosh, whose internationalism is no more meaningful than that of Disney theme parks.

As we have emphasised throughout, our Eutopian agenda means that this is not a grand struggle in the old sense, a fight to overthrow the present and march to a Utopian future. It responds to our new and more open democracy precisely through its refusal to confront and reject. But, despite that lack of a simple mission, its task is no less vital: to create and redistribute architecture across a whole society, to regenerate the Scottish city of daily life as a collective monument to the future of our country. This is an ideal set apart from narrow economistic materialism, yet at the same time one which pragmatically acknowledges the limitations of action at the end of the twentieth century, and the impossibility of authoritarian, fundamentalist or big-government prescriptions. If architecture is truly Scotland's national art, then the revitalisation of our architectural legacy of freedom with order can fittingly symbolise the identity of the new Scottish nation: a nation rooted no longer in a martial unity of serried uniforms and material Progress, but in the richness of place and individual diversity.

Monument to the future: St Mary's Cathedral Song School,
Edinburgh, and chorister pupils at work

NOTES

1. P. Geddes and V. Branford, 'Prefatory Note', *Evergreen*, Autumn 1895, cited in *Edinburgh Review*, 88, Summer 1992, p. 16
2. C. Dickens, *Hard Times* (originally published 1854), 1901 edition, Nelson, London & Edinburgh, p. 27
3. D. Hume, 1770, cited in M. Glendinning, R. MacInnes, A. Mac-Kechnie, *A History of Scottish Architecture* (hereafter *HSA*), Edinburgh University Press, Edinburgh, 1996, p. 147
4. Sir W. Scott, *Old Mortality*, 1816 edition
5. *Glasgow Herald*, 24 November 1858, cited in *Glasgow Architectural Society Proceedings*, 23 February 1859
6. A. Thomson, *Glasgow Architectural Society Proceedings*, 23 February 1859
7. A. Thomson, Haldane Lectures, cited in *HSA*, p. 253
8. Lecture by Werner Sewing, Edinburgh University Architecture Department symposium, 10 May 1998
9. P. Geddes and Colleagues, *A First Visit to the Outlook Tower*, 1906, cited in *Edinburgh Review*, 88, Summer 1992, p. 16
10. Geddes not conservationist: V. Welter, lecture at Duncan of Jordanstone College, 18 November 1997; V. Welter, 'The Republic of Patrick Geddes', *Edinburgh Architecture Research*, 1994, pp. 98–118; V. Welter, 'Patrick Geddes and the City', *Edinburgh Architecture Research*, 1995, pp. 11–30; V. Welter, 'History, Biology and City Design', *Architectural Heritage*, 6, 1996, p. 78. Science of civics: P. Geddes, lecture of 18 December 1912, *Royal Philosophical Society of Glasgow Transactions*. 'To the baser spirits', *Evergreen*, Spring 1895, cited in *Edinburgh Review*, 88, Summer 1992, p. 16
11. P. Womersley, 'Peter Womersley', *RIBA Journal*, May 1969, p. 196
12. D. Lyddon, *Town Theory*, report for Cumbernauld Development Corporation. Roger Emmerson, 'American', *New Towns, New Times, New Themes*, Royal Fine Art Commission for Scotland exhibition text, 1995
13. 'Andy MacMillan Interview', *MacMag*, 19, 1994, p. 24

Notes

14. Patrick Geddes, *Dramatisations of History*, Edinburgh, 1923, p. iv
15. R. Murphy, *Architects' Journal*, 30 November 1995; B. Tindall, 11 February 1997 lecture, Scottish National Portrait Gallery; P. Geddes, *Evergreen*, Spring 1895, cited in *Edinburgh Review*, 88, Summer 1992, p. 16
16. *Proverbs*, 29:18
17. Thucydides, Funeral Oration of Pericles, *Histories*, 2.43
18. Matthew, see *HSA*, p. 385
19. M. Glendinning and S. Muthesius, *Tower Block*, Yale, New Haven, 1994, pp. 237, 235
20. R. Holloway, *Dancing on the Edge*, Fount, London, 1997, and lecture at Cornerstone Cafe, Edinburgh, 1 September 1997, 'They don't just describe . . .', sermon by R. Holloway, 31 May 1998, St Mary's Cathedral, Edinburgh, and interview with M. Glendinning, 28 September 1998
21. P. McMylor, *Alastair MacIntyre*, London, 1994
22. Ian Hamilton Finlay, *Poursuites Revolutionnaires*, 1987. M. Cousins, 'The Wilderness Garden', *Chapman*, 78–9, October 1994, p. 102
23. 'Glasgow 1999', *MacMag* 20, 1995, p. 34, paragraph by S. Stoddart
24. R. Holloway, *Builder*, 5 September 1969
25. J. Ruskin, *The Stones of Venice*, 1851, vol. 1, ch. 2, para. 1 (p. 27 in G. Allen, London, 1902 edition)
26. Thucydides, *Histories*, 1.22
27. C. Willsdon, *Scots Magazine*, February 1993
28. R. H. Matthew, 'The Influences of Environment', lecture to Council of Industrial Design conference, Glasgow, 14 November 1953. R. H. Matthew, 1970: see *HSA*, p. 473
29. S. MacDonald, interview with D. Page, 1998
30. Alois Riegl, *Der Moderne Denkmalkultus, sein Wesen, seine Entstehhung*, Wien, 1903; Very Rev. Graham Forbes, *Magnificat* (magazine of St Mary's Cathedral, Edinburgh), October 1998
31. *Architects' Journal*, 6 March 1997; *Construction Manager*, June 1997
32. Scottish Office Development Department, *National Planning Policy Guidelines*, 1 ('The Planning System'), 1994
33. 'Celebrating at Castlemilk', *Scotland's New Homebuyer*, Spring 1997, p. 54
34. Royal Fine Art Commission for Scotland, *Report* for 1996, Edinburgh, 1998, p. 9
35. *HSA*, p. 462
36. Aase Kleveland (Norwegian Minister of Cultural Affairs), lecture

at Manifesto conference, Roxburghe Hotel, Edinburgh, 11 October 1996

37. *Transactions of the Royal Philosophical Society of Glasgow*, 18 December 1917

38. Europan, *Europan 4 UK*, London, 1996

39. See for example Richard Asbury, *Degeneration to Regeneration*, MA thesis, Edinburgh University Department of Architecture, 1997

40. G. Stamp, *Scotland on Sunday*, 27 April 1997; Andrew MacMillan, *Glasgow Herald*, 22 March 1995

41. Alan Johnston, *A Without State*, 1997; M. Gooding, 'Sense and Sensibility', *Art Monthly*, October 1995, pp. 8–10; Alan Johnston, notes to T. Struth exhibition, *The Looking-Glass City*, at Reiach & Hall, Edinburgh, 1997; Alan Johnston, Fruitmarket Gallery, Edinburgh, 1987, pp. 6–10

42. 'Local Knowledge', *Prospect*, Winter 1997, pp. 19–20

43. R. Parry, 'The Scottish Parliament and Social Policy', *Scottish Affairs*, Summer 1997, p. 37

44. 'Tent in the Meadows', *Herald*, 16 July 1997

LIST OF ILLUSTRATIONS

The square brackets at end of each entry contain the date of the photograph, and copyright information. Captions for paired pictures are put together.

COVER

Clone City/Clydeforth from space. [1990s; Science Photo Library]

CHAPTER 1

Clone City: the landscape of market choice. [1999; M. Glendinning] xii

Clone City: anywhere in Central Scotland. [1999; M. Glendinning] 9

CHAPTER 2

Hopetoun House, late seventeenth/early eighteenth-century planned country estate. [1983; RCAHMS] 18
New Lanark, late eighteenth-century planned industrial village. [1975; RCAHMS] 19

The elite early nineteenth-century Edinburgh suburb: Moray Estate. [1984; RCAHMS] 22
The elite mid-nineteenth-century Glasgow suburb: Woodlands Hill. [1989; RCAHMS] 23

1890s tenements, Gorgie, Edinburgh. [1989; RCAHMS] 30
1960s housing, Tanshall, Glenrothes New Town. [1989; RCAHMS] 31

New university in a park, Stirling, 1960s. [1984; RCAHMS] 36
Housing scheme in landscape, Castlemilk, Glasgow, 1950s–60s. [1991; RCAHMS] 37

1920s cottages and 1960s tower blocks, Knightswood, Glasgow. [1989; RCAHMS] 40
1890s tenements, Dennistoun, Glasgow. [1990; RCAHMS] 41

East-coast historic burgh: Dunbar. [1978; RCAHMS] 46
West-coast New Town: Cumbernauld. [1991; RCAHMS] 47

High Street and Parliament Square, Edinburgh Old Town. [1990; RCAHMS] 60
Wyndford, Glasgow: planned redevelopment by the Scottish Special Housing Association, 1961–9. [1989; RCAHMS] 61

CHAPTER 3

Seafield Colliery, Kirkcaldy, 1960s winding tower. [1988; RCAHMS] 67
Linlithgow Palace (fifteenth–seventeenth-century royal seat of the Stuart kings). [1983; RCAHMS] 68

Stirling Castle. [1974; RCAHMS] 75
St James Centre and New St Andrew's House, Edinburgh. [1985; RCAHMS] 76

Niddry Bing, Broxburn: the landscape of nineteenth-century shale mining. [1991; RCAHMS] 79
The King's Knot, Stirling: Renaissance pleasure garden. [1990; RCAHMS] 80

Muirhouse, Edinburgh: 1960s outer-suburban social housing complex. [1991; RCAHMS] 87
Corstorphine, Edinburgh: 1900s–30s outer-suburban private housing. [1991; RCAHMS] 88

Gartcosh Steel Mill, Lanarkshire. [1991; RCAHMS] 95
Haddington, historic East Lothian burgh. [1990; RCAHMS] 96

Glenboig, c. 1930 working-class housing scheme: urban order in the rural landscape. [1991; RCAHMS] 105
Netherlee, c. 1900 middle-class housing: suburban order in the urban landscape. [1989; RCAHMS] 106

CHAPTER 4

The Forth Valley at Stirling. [1949; Crow & Rodgers, Stirling] 112
Clydeforth: map from the Mears Report, 1948; Scottish Office] 112
The Clyde Valley at Greenock. [1989; RCAHMS] 112

Inner Ring Road, St George's Cross, Glasgow. [1990; RCAHMS] 116
Stirling Castle and the Wallace Monument. [1984; RCAHMS] 117

List of Illustrations

Central Leith. [1991; RCAHMS] 124
Central Dumbarton. [1989; RCAHMS] 125

Linlithgow: Forth Valley heritage in landscape. [1990; RCAHMS] 128
Grangemouth: Forth Valley industry in landscape. [1991; RCAHMS] 129

Rails down the Clyde: Glasgow Central Station. [1990; RCAHMS] 134
Wemyss Bay Station. [1988; RCAHMS] 135

CHAPTER 5

1960s planned housing, Craigshill, Livingston New Town. [1989; RCAHMS] 139
1870s planned housing, Wester Coates Estate, Edinburgh. [1988; RCAHMS] 141

Planned burgh, Gifford, East Lothian. [1978; RCAHMS] 145
Replanned burgh, Glasgow Townhead Interchange, 1960s–70s. [1990; RCAHMS] 147

Livingston New Town, built from 1962. [1988; RCAHMS] 151
Glenrothes New Town, built from 1951. [1988; RCAHMS] 153

Glasgow city centre grid. [1990; RCAHMS] 155
Edinburgh city centre, old (foreground) and new (background). [1993; RCAHMS] 157

Pollokshields, Glasgow, nineteenth-century villa suburb. [1991; RCAHMS] 161
Early nineteenth-century New Town, Greenock. [1989; RCAHMS] 163

East Kilbride New Town, built from 1947. [1989; RCAHMS] 167
Haddington historic burgh. [1985; RCAHMS] 169

Homes in landscape: Sighthill multi-storey project, Glasgow, 1963–9. [1991; RCAHMS] 173
Democracy in landscape: Lanark county headquarters, Hamilton, 1959–64. [1990; RCAHMS] 175

CHAPTER 6

Satellite photograph of Clydeforth. [1990s; Science Photo Library] 178–9

Irvine New Town, built from 1968. [1988; RCAHMS] 182
Cumbernauld New Town, built from 1958. [1988; RCAHMS] 183

Clydeside centres: Paisley town centre. [1991; RCAHMS] 184
Cumbernauld, Seafar housing area. [1991; RCAHMS] 185

Street crossing, Edinburgh New Town. [1985; RCAHMS] 188
River crossing, Kincardine-on-Forth. [1988; RCAHMS] 189

Edinburgh Royal Infirmary, 1870s–1970s. [1989; RCAHMS] 192
Grangemouth Refinery. [1991; RCAHMS] 193

North Edinburgh. [1988; RCAHMS] 196
South Glasgow. [1988; RCAHMS] 197

Central Greenock. [1989; RCAHMS] 202
Outer Motherwell: the Muirhouse housing project (mid-1960s) and the
Ravenscraig steelworks. [1989; RCAHMS] 203

Port Glasgow centre. [1989; RCAHMS] 206
The Gorbals and Glasgow city centre. [1990; RCAHMS] 207

Dunoon pier. [1989; RCAHMS] 212
Clydebank shipyards. [1988; RCAHMS] 213

CHAPTER 7

Monument to reconciliation: Pope John Paul II meets the Moderator of
the Church of Scotland in the courtyard of New College (interim home
of the new parliament from 1999) in 1982. [1982; Scottish Catholic
Archive/Pontificia Felici] 216

Monument to the future: St Mary's Song School, Edinburgh (decorated
by Phoebe Traquair, 1888–92) and chorister pupils at work. [1999;
RCAHMS] 222–3

INDEX

Abercrombie, P., 39, 42, 126, 190, 208
Aberdeen, 25, 100, 120, 162
Adam, Robert, 4, 20, 85
Amsterdam, 143, 149
Arbor Saeculorum, 33, 50, 56, 58
Arcade Architects, 190
architectural form, 2, 43–4, 48, 53
architectural space, 43–4, 150, 152, 156, 160, 165, 172
Aristotle, 33
art, 74, 97
Athens, 64, 66
Austria, 218

Baines, Mark, 160
Barrhead, 210
Baxter, Clark & Paul, 194
Bearsden, 199
Beaux-Arts, 39, 42, 44, 199
Begg, Ian, 51
Belgium, 20
Benson & Forsyth, 140
Berlin, 107, 120, 158
brick building, 2, 7, 54, 86, 92, 97, 102, 150, 164, 170, 186, 199
Britain, 13, 17
brownfield land, 148–9, 190–1, 195, 201, 204
Broxburn, 79
Bruce, Robert, 39, 44, 198–9
Bryce, D., 219
building industry, 21, 89, 93–4, 97–8
Bunton, Sam, 48
Burn, W., 17
Burnet, J. J., 28, 39
business park *see* commercial buildings

capitalism, 3–8, 17, 20–1, 29, 32, 45, 48, 51–5, 65–6, 69–72, 78, 84, 89, 91, 93–4, 98–9, 102–3, 108, 111, 123, 195, 198, 204, 220
Cardross, 43
Catholic Church, 72, 219
Central Belt, 6, 7, 33, 58, 100–1, 106, 109, 113–14, 118, 120, 123, 170
central government *see* government
Church of Scotland, 17, 72, 219
city centre *see* inner city
city region *see* conurbation
class *see* society
Clerk, Sir J., 27
cloning, 5, 7, 15, 32, 48, 220
Clyde, River, 6, 39, 127, 130, 194, 208–11, 218
Clyde Valley Regional Plan, 39, 42, 100, 126, 132, 195, 198–200
Clydebank, 213
Clydeforth, 33, 59, 112–13, 118, 123, 126, 130–2, 146, 149–50, 157, 177, 179, 186–7, 199, 210, 214
Coatbridge, 21
Coley, N., 54
commercial buildings, 1, 154, 172, 187, 211
commodification *see* capitalism
community, 7, 26, 45, 51, 64–5, 69–70, 73, 78, 82–3, 85–6, 91, 92, 109, 111, 120, 158, 166, 168, 205, 210
conservation *see* heritage
conurbation, 6–7, 16, 33, 35, 58–9, 112–14, 118–32, 140, 146, 186–7, 208–14, 220
council housing *see* social housing

Cumbernauld New Town, 44, 47, 108, 177, 180, 183, 185

Dean of Guild, 17, 99
democracy, 6–8, 57–9, 63–6, 72, 74, 77–8, 81–2, 85–6, 91, 102–3, 107, 111, 217–20
demography *see* society
density, 21, 126, 143–4, 149, 158, 160, 177, 180
Disruption, 17
DOCOMOMO, 57
Dumbarton, 125
Dunbar, 46
Dundee, 164, 168
Dunoon, 211, 212
Dysart, 164

East Kilbride New Town, 39, 166–7, 177, 180, 208
Edinburgh, 25–7, 34, 42, 78, 113, 122–3, 126–7, 130, 132, 138, 146, 148, 157, 164, 180, 187, 190, 196
  Calton Hill, 4
  Corstorphine, 88
  Edinburgh Park, 172
  Gorgie, 30
  Gyle, 180
  High Street, 60
  Holyrood, 187, 190
  Leith, 124, 159, 187, 191
  Lothian Road, 187
  Moray Estate, 22, 99
  Mound, 24, 219
  Muirhouse, 87
  Museum of Scotland, 140
  New College, 216, 219
  New Town, 27–8, 32, 50, 78, 152, 164, 188
  Old Town, 27–8, 32, 35, 152, 190
  Royal Infirmary, 191
  South East Wedge, 191
  St James Centre, 76
  St Mary's Cathedral and Song School, 85, 222–3
  Wester Coates, 141
  Wester Hailes, 82, 168

education, 84–6, 111, 219, 222–3
Elder & Cannon, 154, 160, 204–5
England, 13, 29, 50, 94, 148, 159
Erskine, 181
Europan, 70
Eutopia, 33, 35, 56, 108, 114–15, 119, 140, 146, 171, 177, 200, 220

family *see* society
Findhorn, 81
Finlay, Ian Hamilton, 73–4
firmitas, 12, 74, 84
Fordism, 38, 48, 52
form *see* architectural form
Forth, River, 6, 39, 127, 191, 194
France, 13
Fraser, M., 190
Functionalism *see* Modernism
fundamentalism, 71, 73, 113–14, 123, 138, 140, 143, 146, 154, 156, 186, 204, 221

Gartcosh, 95, 210
Geddes, Patrick, 8, 32–4, 42, 50, 56, 58–9, 78, 91, 104, 106, 118, 123, 201
Germany, 13, 43
Gibson, P., 64
Gifford, 145
Gillespie, Neil, 191
Glasgow, 25–7, 38, 42, 78, 91, 113, 122–3, 126–7, 130, 132, 146, 149, 154–6, 158, 160, 164, 180, 194–5, 197–201, 204–5, 208, 210
  Art Lover's House, 51–2
  Blythswood, 21, 152
  Burrell Gallery, 50
  Castlemilk, 37, 168, 195, 208
  Central Station, 134
  Darnley, 170
  Dennistoun, 41
  Drumchapel, 168
  Easterhouse, 82, 166, 210
  Glasgow Architectural Society, 25
  Glasgow Development Agency, 149
  Glasgow Empire Exhibition, 44
  Glasgow School of Art, 74

Index

Gorbals, 44, 49, 180, 204–5, 207
Homes for the Future project,
    205, 208
Inner Ring Road, 116, 147, 201
Kelvinside, 82
Knightswood, 40
Lighthouse, 86
Maryhill Corridor, 201
Merchant City, 201
Municipal Buildings, 39
Pollok, 210
Pollokshields, 161
Sighthill, 173
Woodlands Hill, 23
Wyndford, 61, 20
Glenboig, 105
Glenrothes New Town, 31, 131, 153,
    171, 194
globalisation see capitalism
Gourock, 210–11
government, 3, 17, 26, 38–9, 51, 58,
    64–6, 70–1, 77, 89–90, 93,
    98–111, 120, 130, 177,
    199–200, 217–21
Grangemouth, 129, 192, 194
green belt, 100, 121–2, 149–50, 165,
    190–1, 208
greenfield land, 148–9, 191
Greenock, 112, 163, 202, 210
'GRO-Grants', 101

Haddington, 96, 169, 194
Hamilton, 171, 175
Harding, D., 74
Helensburgh, 211
Henket, Hubert-Jan, 57
heritage, 2, 27, 34, 45, 50–1, 54,
    56–9, 74, 77–8, 81, 83–4, 86,
    89–90, 108–11, 138, 187, 190,
    201
high density see density
Historic Scotland, 109–10
historical landscape see heritage
historicism, 16–29, 48–9, 63, 103,
    137, 142, 144, 218
Holloway, Richard, 73, 81
home rule, 5–6, 77, 90, 102, 104,
    107–8, 111, 122, 217–21

Hope, John, 190
Hopetoun House, 18
housebuilding see building industry
housing scheme see social housing
Hume, David, 4
Hurd, Robert, 45

identity, 5, 14, 51, 57–8, 69–70,
    72–4, 78, 82–3, 85, 91–2, 120,
    127, 137, 168, 205, 217–21
imperialism, 13, 17, 20, 28, 199, 218
Improvement, Age of, 16–17, 20, 137
inequality, 28–9, 43, 63–5, 70, 81–2,
    137, 211, 219
inner city, 1, 35, 49, 104, 113, 123,
    138, 144, 150–64, 181, 187,
    201, 204–5, 208
inner suburb see inner city
Iona Community, 72
Ireland, 102, 110, 159
Irvine New Town, 131, 177, 181–2,
    186

Jameson, F., 4
Johnson-Marshall, Percy, 42
Johnston, Alan, 4
Joiner, Rob, 92

Kincardine-on-Forth, 189
Kirkcaldy, 67
Kirkintilloch, 210
Knox, John, 219

laissez-faire see capitalism
landscape, 21, 44, 115, 121, 127,
    146, 165, 172, 180, 191, 210
Leeuwarden, 4
liberalism see capitalism
Linlithgow, 68, 128
Livingston New Town, 1, 39, 150,
    177, 194
local authority see government
low density see density

MacDonald, S., 86
McGurn, Logan, Duncan & Opfer,
    160
Macintyre, Alasdair, 73

McKeown Alexander, 208
Mackintosh, C. R., 43, 49, 51, 53–4,
    84, 181, 201, 220
McLachlan, Ewen and Fiona, 180
MacMillan, Andrew, 53
MacRae, Ken, 160
Mactaggart & Mickel, 93, 97, 208
Mar, Lord, 27
market *see* capitalism
Mather, R., 205
Matthew, Robert, 42, 50, 54, 59, 64,
    66, 78, 85, 91, 164, 190, 205,
    208
Mears, F., 39, 42, 104, 112, 126,
    177, 194
Merrylees Grierson & Robertson,
    209
Miralles, E., 53
Mitchell, Sydney, 28
mixed use, 3, 114, 152, 154, 160,
    165–6, 181, 204
modern civilisation, 12–15, 25, 27–9,
    34, 50, 58, 72, 74, 77, 94, 118,
    201
Modern Movement *see* Modernism
Modernism, 38–59, 63–6, 69, 77–8,
    85, 98–9, 103, 108, 114–15,
    118–19, 126–7, 138, 142, 144,
    152, 158, 160, 162, 172, 174,
    186, 204–5
modernity *see* modern civilisation
Morris, W., 50, 56, 89
Motherwell, 21, 203, 209
Murphy, R., 190
Murray, Allan, 4

nation, 6–7, 29, 69, 140, 217–21
national identity *see* nation
Neotechnic civilisation, 33, 35, 42,
    77, 82–3, 220
Netherlands, 99, 103, 130, 159
Netherlee, 106
New Lanark, 19
new towns, 3, 39, 49, 99, 103, 108,
    114, 126, 130, 138, 149, 177,
    180–6, 191, 194–5, 208–10
Norway, 110

oligarchy, 16–17, 63, 78, 90, 97, 99
Ossian, 27
outer city, 1, 21, 34, 49, 104, 113,
    119–20, 122, 127, 140, 144,
    146, 165–74, 187, 194–5, 199,
    208–11, 214

Paisley, 168, 184, 210
Palaeotechnic civilisation, 32, 35, 42,
    81
parliament, 6, 122, 218–20
Parry, Richard, 217
participation *see* democracy
periphery *see* outer city
planning, town and country, 21, 33,
    35, 42, 44, 49, 58, 100–11,
    120–1, 123–32, 137, 148, 165,
    190–1, 195, 198, 200–1, 219
Playfair, W., 20, 24, 219
Pope John Paul II, 216, 219
Port Glasgow, 206, 210–11
Postmodernism, 4, 16, 45, 48–54,
    56–7, 71, 73, 78–91, 108, 118,
    138, 143, 146, 150, 158, 201
poverty *see* inequality
Presbyterianism *see* religion
Prestwick Airport, 132
Prince Charles, 66
privacy *see* society
private transport *see* transport
progress, concept of, 4, 11, 16, 26,
    34, 38, 45, 48, 50–1, 55, 57–9,
    69–72, 77, 81, 83, 120, 221
Protestantism *see* religion
public art *see* art
public buildings, 140, 152, 171, 174,
    218–19
public housing *see* social housing
public transport *see* transport

Randstad, 120
Rebois, D., 120
redevelopment, 24, 26, 28, 34, 39,
    44, 48, 195, 201, 204–5, 209
Reiach, A., 54, 171
Reiach & Hall, 191
religion, 17, 20, 25–6, 72–3, 89, 216,
    218–19

Index

Renfrew, 210
Riegl, Alois, 89
ring road *see* transport
RMJM, 208
roads *see* transport
Rogan, P., 64
Romantic Movement, 27–8, 118
Rothesay, 211
Royal Fine Art Commission for
    Scotland, 100–1, 109–10
Ruskin, J., 82
Rutherford, Roan, 181

Salmon, James, 25
Saltire Society, 45
Scott, F. C., 166
Scott, Sir W., 25, 27
Scottish Episcopal Church, 73
Scottish Homes, 97, 101, 110
Scottish Special Housing Association,
    180, 205
sculpture *see* art
Second Vatican Council, 72
Shaw, Geoff, 72
Sitte, C., 34
social exclusion *see* inequality
social housing, 38–9, 44, 48–9, 70,
    82, 91, 93, 97, 101, 148, 156,
    159, 166, 168, 170, 180, 194,
    211
socialism, 35, 45, 64–5, 70–1, 81, 92,
    198
society, 7, 15, 21, 29, 44–5, 48, 51,
    53, 57–9, 63–6, 69, 71, 73,
    78–82, 85, 89–91, 97–9, 137,
    140, 142, 148, 156, 158, 160,
    162, 205, 208, 217–21
space *see* architectural space
Spence, B., 43, 49, 53, 204–5
Stamp, Gavin, 168
state, the *see* government
Steel, James, 91
Stevenson, R. L., 32
Stewart, F., 91
Stirling, 36, 75, 80, 112, 117
Stoddart, A., 74
stone building, 24, 115, 118, 164, 191
Strathclyde Regional Council, 85, 199

suburb *see* outer city
Sweden, 111

Tait, T. S., 39, 42, 44, 48
Taylorism, 38, 52
tenement, 26, 29–30, 42, 49, 99,
    156–62, 164, 166, 190–5, 198,
    204–5, 211
terrace housing, 159–60
Thomson, Alexander, 26
Thucydides, 84
Tindall, Frank, 127, 194
tower block, 42, 44, 48, 49, 51, 86,
    144, 152, 162, 164, 171, 180,
    204–5, 211
town centre *see* inner city
transport, 2, 44, 104, 131–2, 142,
    148, 149, 200, 209, 211, 214
Traquair, Phoebe, 85

uenustas, 12, 43–4, 74, 84
Ungless & Latimer, 190
United States of America, 13, 20
urban village, 3, 158, 165, 181, 191,
    199, 205
Ushida & Findlay, 208
utilitas, 12, 74, 84
Utopia, 11, 14, 16, 25, 45, 48–9,
    54–6, 59, 66, 71, 77, 114, 119,
    138, 168, 220

Villa Savoye, 54
VINEX Plan, 130, 148
Vitruvius, 12–14, 49, 74

Wagner, O., 218
Welsh, Irvine, 3
Welter, Volker, 225
Wemyss Bay, 135
Wheeler & Sproson, 45, 127, 164,
    171, 194
Womersley, P., 43
Wren, G., 181
Wren Rutherford, 181, 208

zoning, 107, 127, 138, 181, 187,
    198–9